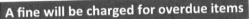

Published by
British Agencies for Adoption and Fostering
(BAAF)
Skyline House
200 Union Street
London SE1 0LX

Charity registration 275689

© BAAF 1999

ISBN 1 873868 69 3

Typeset by Aldgate Press
Printed by Lavenham Press

Introduction

DONAL GILTINAN

As the world enters the third millennium it is appropriate to reflect on the development and well being of children and young people who will be the first citizens of this new era. The symbolism is irresistible. A new century, a new millennium: a time to take stock of the past, to look forward to the future with hope and purpose. This collection of ten papers represents a cross-section of the empirical research and thinking about childhood generally and looked after children in particular at the end of the twentieth century. When we review its treatment of its child citizens during the course of the century we are tempted to say, 'How could we possibly have done that and thought it was right?'. For example, separating children from the perceived corrupting influence of their kith and kin and sending them in their shiploads to Australia and America. Yet, there can be little doubt about the integrity and the genuineness of the philanthropists who were the founders of modern child care.

If these papers were to be reviewed 100 years from now, will we too be judged as well-intentioned but somewhat misguided? The structure of our society is constantly changing and the patterns and processes of how each generation cares for its children present us with new challenges and new insights. In one way or another, these papers deal with our emerging wisdom and knowledge about a group of children who cannot be nurtured within their birth families.

Clifford in his paper reminds us that the theoretical framework underpinning social work assessment in adoption and fostering is absent or inadequate. Brophy's paper on expert assessments in court proceedings suggests that, contrary to much received wisdom, the majority of cases do not contain a huge amount of competing evidence. Thoburn in her reflective overview of the impact of research acknowledges the cyclical nature of the relationship between research theory and practice. Rushton's paper on the impact of social work intervention in the preparation and support of late placements should give pause for thought to family placement workers who expect experienced families to be better used to dealing with challenging behaviours. Despite the lessons of history about separating children from their nearest and dearest, Mullender's paper on siblings informs us that sibling separation is still common, with much of our practice being well-meaning but confused. Elgar and Head's paper on living with siblings who have been sexually abused points out some of the implications of abuse for the assessment of children and reminds us that many carers were unprepared for the consequences of sexual abuse. Kirton and Woodger's paper on their research from a pilot project on the experiences of transracial adoption is a timely reminder of the cultural strengths of our minority ethnic families that have been overlooked or undervalued by the predominant culture.

There is an interesting argument about whether law and policy lead social beliefs and practice or whether laws are shaped and therefore pursue the social beliefs of the society it regulates. There can be little doubt about the importance or the influence of research and social policy especially in the realm of children and children's lives. Children, however, have made a shadowy appearance on the stage of social policy and have been largely represented there by an ambivalent press of narrow pages and some concerned adults with broad minds.

Child-centred policy distinguishes itself from child care policy by the extent to which it is based on the premise that children have an inherent value in their own right and not merely or even mainly as future adults. In our time there has been a tendency to "problematise" the range of meanings with which childhood has been invested. Childhood has been presented as difficult or vulnerable or demanding; all somewhat negative images of childhood.

This selection of papers from an information-rich symposium will leave the reader in no doubt about the dynamism and evolution of knowledge about all our child citizens. When we think we have reached the fullness of knowledge we have stopped thinking and we do our children a great disservice.

Some reflections on the impact of research on the practice of permanent family placement

JUNE THOBURN
Dean of School of
Social Work
University of East Anglia

The relationship between research and practice

For the purpose of this introductory contribution, **child placement practice** will be split into its three main components:

- assessment and making decisions about the different components of a placement;

- assessment and approval of prospective adopters and foster parents;

- the helping process (including casework, groupwork, therapy, negotiation, advocacy and emotional and practical support);

Help in its various forms has to be available to birth family members, the members of the new family, and the adopted or fostered child before placement, during the matching process, at the time of placement, during the Court proceedings, during childhood and in later life.

Research will be considered under two headings:

- evaluative or predictive studies which seek to tease out "what works";

- descriptive research which may provide facts and figures, may describe elements of practice, or may give accounts of the placement process as experienced by birth parents, the young people or their substitute parents.

Statistical or evaluative studies have had more of an impact on practice than have descriptive studies. Consequently research has had a bigger impact on the decision making process than on practice. This has been the case especially since 1985 when the first major Department of Health research overview (Department of Health and Social Security, 1985) had a significant impact on the Children Act 1989 and its accompanying practice guidance.

It is less evident that researchers have had an impact on helping methods and the child placement process. Here we need to acknowledge the cyclical nature of the relationship between research, theory and practice. Family placement has been fortunate in the quality of the professional workers (paediatricians, psychiatrists, lawyers, therapists and social workers) who have been drawn to this area of practice. I think no one would quibble if I include here Jane Rowe, Phillida Sawbridge, Claudia Jewett, and going back a bit, Clare Winnicott amongst social work practitioners; Donald Winnicott, James and Joyce Robertson and Vera Fahlberg from psychiatry; and Brenda Hoggett from law. Their creativity has led to innovations in practice and changes in the law which have then been evaluated by researchers whose findings have fed back into practice. In the process, some practice theories, and some research findings have been discarded, sometimes for pragmatic reasons such as lack of resources, sometimes because the interests of one of the major groups involved in adoption might have taken precedence over those of another group. At times in our history the interests of adopters have appeared to win out over those of children and birth parents; at other times children's interests have taken precedence.

There is, then, a dialogue but also a tension between researchers and practitioners. In part this is because practitioners tend to remember the difficult cases. But, in an area so emotive as adoption which touches the lives of the rich as well as the poor, and some who appear to the media and general public as more "deserving" than others, there is a risk that "hard cases make bad laws" or bad "practice wisdom". Researchers, on the other hand, tend to make generalisations and predictions based on the "average" – what is most likely to happen to the majority of children of a particular age or with a particular disability, placed in a particular type of placement There will always be exceptions and almost every family placement worker will know of one. For example, one of the few consistent conclusions from research is that success rates are lower if there is an "own grown" child similar in age or younger than the child placed, but most adoption workers will be able to come up with exceptions to that particular "rule" – I can certainly think of one or two highly successful adoptions which have succeeded in those circumstances.

Some examples are now given of ways in which research has influenced first of all decision making, and then processes and practice. The list is not exhaustive. The examples chosen appear to me to be particularly topical or to illustrate particular debates about practice. I shall start with those issues where the clearest links can be seen between research findings and changes in practice.*

The impact of research findings on decision making

Different sorts of families for different sorts of children
The clearest example of researchers evaluating innovations in practice, and practice then building on research, concerns the recruitment of substitute parents for older children in care. American and British family placement workers demonstrated in the 1980s that a wide range of parents and family types could meet the needs of children who have special needs. The result is that, despite the pronouncements of politicians that married couples in "traditional" families are to be preferred, children have been placed in increasing numbers with single parents who may live on their own or may have a "live in" or a "live out" partner. Evaluative and descriptive studies (see footnote) have provided support for this practice.

Pursuing this theme of the types of families who can successfully provide substitute care for children, there has been a marked change in practice towards the placement of more children with relatives, and for placements of children well settled with short-term foster carers to be confirmed as "permanent". In these circumstances, an earlier tendency amongst social workers to prefer "stranger" placements has been reversed, largely as a

---

* In this short overview it is invidious to pick out a few amongst the many research studies so detailed references are not given. For those who wish to track these ideas back to the evidence, the sources are to be found in Sellick, C. and Thoburn, J. (1996) *What works in family placement?*, Barnardo's; and Thoburn, J. (1999) 'Trends in foster care and adoption' in Stevenson, O. (Ed) *Child Welfare in the UK, 1948 – 1998*, Oxford: Blackwell Science, pp 121-155.

result of the evidence coming from child development and family placement researchers.

When we consider the placement of children of minority ethnic origin, the research is less clear cut. Whilst qualitative evidence and smaller consumer studies, particularly those which consider ethnic pride and identity, weight the evidence on the side of matched placements, when larger scale studies use placement breakdown rates as the outcome measure, no differences are found between ethnically "matched" placements and placements with white families. Despite the lack of firm quantitative evidence, the congruence between the findings from small scale studies and social work values has shifted practice to such an extent that it is now rare for children to be placed transracially (other than those coming from overseas). In this instance, research has played only a small part in the moving from the bottom of the "hierarchy of need" to somewhere near the top, the child's need to be placed with a family who matches as near as possible his or her own ethnic origin. Social work values, "practice wisdom" and the voices of some transracially placed young people have played a bigger part than research in this change.

Post placement contact with birth families

In contrast, research has played a much more significant part in the recognition of the importance of continuing contact with members of the birth family. The need for birth family contact after placement with substitute parents, which was also down at the bottom of the "hierarchy of needs", has moved up somewhere towards the middle since the publication of research findings which have concluded that continuing contact with members of the birth family is either a protective or a neutral factor for the majority of children. It is now quite rare for children to be placed with substitute parents without the birth parents and substitute parents having met, and, so far as older children are concerned, some element of face to face contact after placement with at least one adult member of the birth family is more likely than not.

However, when it comes to children under three, although the totally closed model of adoption has been replaced by a more open model, contact with birth parents and other adult relative is mainly indirect via a third party or "letter box" arrangement. There is, however, no evidence that indirect contact makes a greater contribution to the long term well-being of the children, the birth parent, or the adopters than direct contact. Small scale studies tend to contradict each other in this respect and considerably more research is needed.

It is not therefore immediately understandable why a strong position has been taken by practitioners that for older children "direct" contact is more appropriate and that for younger placed children "indirect" contact is more appropriate. Such qualitative research as exists suggests that direct contact is more straightforward for younger placed than for older placed children. This is because the younger children have fewer difficulties in settling well with adoptive families and therefore are more able to use the contact in an uncomplicated way to gain a realistic sense of identity and biography.

The research on placement with siblings was highlighted in *Patterns and Outcomes in Child Placement* (Department of Health, 1989) and had its impact on the high profile of siblings in the Guidance which accompanied the Children Act 1989. More strenuous attempts are now made to place children together with their siblings. However, my involvement in practice as an expert witness or consultant in complex adoption cases suggests that pragmatic considerations often come in here. This is also an area where there may be conflict between the wishes and needs of potential adopters and the needs of children. There is a tendency to split off the youngest children in a larger sibling group and place them separately with childless adopters on the waiting list, including some who are reluctant to have ongoing contact with any member of the birth family.

The "conduit" theory sometimes comes into decisions about sibling contact, in that sometimes, if older children are having contact with a birth parent, it is decided that there should be no contact between the older sibling and younger siblings placed for adoption in case the older sibling acts as a conduit for information about the birth parents. There is nothing in research which would indicate whether or not this practice is likely to be in the interests of either the older or the younger children. From my work as an expert witness, I am aware that it can cause extreme distress to the older children who tend to be more aware than their younger brothers and sisters of the possible long-term impact of this loss. They may also be harmed by having to make a choice between remaining in contact with their birth parents, or with their siblings. There is some evidence from qualitative studies of adopted adults that a proportion of the younger children themselves will regret having been separated from their older siblings as they grow into adulthood.

On a related issue, the view is often expressed by psychiatrists or psychologists who act as consultants in complex child care cases that children placed from families where there has been sexual abuse should not retain contact either with their siblings or their birth parents or other relatives. This appears to be based on clinical practice since there is no outcome research to support this blanket conclusion. The research on continuing parental and sibling contact is based on populations of children placed some years ago who had been physically maltreated or neglected. However, unless sexual abuse is a very new phenomenon, which most experts doubt, it must be assumed that a proportion of the children in those cohorts had also been sexually assaulted or come from families where sexual maltreatment was a part of the pattern of family life. The evidence on this question is thin and inconclusive, and does not justify blanket policies either in favour or against continuing parental and sibling contact. Clinical accounts and smaller qualitative studies suggest that decisions in such cases should be taken carefully in the light of individual circumstances, including the nature of the maltreatment, the identity of the abuser, whether it is the abused child or a non-abused sibling who is being planned for, and any other protective and risk factors in the situation.

Legal routes to permanence

Finally, in this section on decision making, I pick out the issue of the respective merits of long-term or permanent foster care placement with a view to a Residence Order or placement for adoption as alternative routes to permanent substitute family placement. Here research appears to have had very little impact on practice. Quantitative studies, with large enough numbers to control for the age and difficulty of the children to be placed, find no statistically significant difference in breakdown rates between children with similar backgrounds placed for adoption and those placed in permanent foster care. However, practice and government pronouncements adhere to the view that adoption is to be preferred, and that long-term or permanent foster placement is a placement of last resort.

Qualitative research studies indicate that for some children, especially those who have had multiple placements and are made anxious by social work visits and reviews, adoption or a Residence Order, which transfer parental responsibility from the local authority to the substitute parents, are to be preferred over remaining in the care of the local authority. The advantages of legal adoption for the youngest children who have spent little time with their birth parents are also well documented. However, studies of long-term foster care indicate that some children who join their substitute families soon after becoming "looked after", perhaps after only one other placement, greatly value social work visits and have no sense of *im*permanence. This is also the case with some of their foster parents. This research tends to be ignored in favour of an all-encompassing statement (frequently repeated by politicians and in the press) that being accommodated or in care is inevitably unwelcome and harmful to children.

Similarly, for some substitute parents only adoption will give the sense of security which is important to them. But for some (including many black and Asian families) foster care or Residence Orders make more sense to their world views about how to help children and families, and for others *either* foster care, Residence Orders *or* adoption will be considered appropriate if the choice is made in the interests of the individual child's needs and circumstances. There are many clues within the research about the appropriate choice of legal status. This research is not clearly flagged up on the Looking After Children (Department of Health, 1995) forms which do not list Residence Orders within the choice of legal options when decisions about long-term plans are to be made.

Another adverse consequence of seeing adoption as the "gold standard" of permanent placement and anything else as inferior is that inadequate attention has been given to ways of ensuring that children in long-term foster placements *do* have a sense of permanence, and that Residence Orders are strengthened in appropriate cases to emphasise the "family for life" nature of the arrangement. A single amendment to the Children Act making this possible is long overdue. The message may be getting through, however, in that the Quality Protects standards include long-term foster care as a positive goal.

Instead of improving the position for children who need to be looked after on a long-term basis, some practitioners collude with pressure groups, politicians and the media in perpetuating the myth that being looked after by the local authority is synonymous with "languishing" and "drift", constant movement, and inevitable long-term failure in later life. The new guidance on adoption appears to be so negative about the way in which children are looked after that it aims to have the adopters ready and waiting the moment the Care Order is made. Whilst this is appropriate for most of the small minority of babies to be placed, it is entirely inappropriate for older children for whom careful assessment and consultation with parents, close relatives and the children themselves are essential prior to the choice of placement and before decisions are made about the nature of any future contact with siblings and adult birth relatives.

The tendency to ignore the research on the benefits of long-term or permanent foster care for some children already increases the extent of delay or multiple moves because a foster placement tends not to be sought until all avenues have been explored in seeking adopters. For those children for whom a sense of permanence is more important than the legal status, a policy which seeks *either* foster parents *or* adopters at the same time will succeed in placing more children more quickly with permanent substitute families.

The impact of research on therapeutic and support services

Examples are easier to find when practice has *ignored* the findings from research than the other way round.

There is a clash between child development research on attachment and separation and some practice at the time of placement. It is still not uncommon for contact to be terminated or severely curtailed with parents and relatives whose company the child enjoyed in order to 'give time for attachments with the new family to form'. Child development theory would suggest that to inflict upon a child the short-term pain and possible long-term harm which comes from the severing of an intimate (even if problematic) relationship for the child is not likely to be conducive to that child being in the frame of mind to enter enthusiastically into a new relationship. In behavioural terms, to associate something negative (an experience of loss) with something which it is hoped will be a positive experience (joining a new family) is to invite difficulties.

Another example is to be found from practice with birth parents at the time of placement. The small amount of research on birth parents suggests that workers should concentrate not on "counselling" and "grief work" but rather on support, advocacy, and practical help to assist them in working out what role they can play in their child's future life, and then in carrying through that role. Help to come to terms with their loss is still important, but the work is different from the days when the total severance model of adoption was the norm. Helping parents to write the letters, birthday cards, or prepare for the phone calls or visits may lead on to the supportive and therapeutic relationship which can help them subsequently to surmount the challenges of their role as parents without children.

Turning to post-placement work with substitute parents, several studies have concluded that it is the family placement worker who is best placed to provide the support to the new family, with the child's worker remaining more in the background. Whilst this is the most usual model of service for the voluntary agencies, the opposite is usually the case when children are placed by local authority workers. In some cases this will be the right thing to do, but this custom and practice should be looked at more carefully to see if guidelines can be reached as to the model best suited in different cases.

Perhaps the most worrying area in which practice has not taken on board the messages from research is in the nature of social work and the review process when children remain in permanent foster families or are placed initially as foster children prior to an application to adopt. Several studies indicated that once it has been decided that a foster family will be the child's "family for life", the review process should take on a different form. Recent research on children's involvement in reviews adds strength to this proposition. However, many authorities do not adapt their review process and social work practice to acknowledge the difference between a permanent foster placement and a temporary one and thus themselves engender a sense of impermanence.

A further example is the tendency for leaving care team workers to attend the review of the child in long-term foster care who is reaching the age of 16. This risks giving the impression that it is expected that the young person will soon be moving on. As the Utting report (Utting, 1997) has so forcefully reminded us, good parents expect to continue to provide aspects of parenting until their children are well into their 20s, and most long-term foster parents are no exception. Whilst some foster parents and young people are beginning to feel a need to have more space between them and would welcome a discussion of whether remaining in close contact but living in supported lodgings would be appropriate, to build this into routine practice can have a destabilising effect.

To conclude this introductory chapter, I make no apology for the emphasis I have placed on foster care as a route to permanence. The majority of children who are looked after for substantial periods of time are in their middle years, have experienced maltreatment or other trauma, and have complicated relationships with birth family members or previous carers. Whilst some will be successfully placed for adoption, most, if they are to find high quality parenting and long-term caring relationships, will find them in a foster family. Whether they are adopted or fostered, there is a high risk at the present time that they will experience multiple moves in short-term foster or residential care *before* they are placed. The clearest message from research is that short-term foster *caring* and longer term foster *parenting* must be given the highest priority both for research and for improvements in practice. I have an anxiety that the totally appropriate drive to move children more quickly into substitute family placements will be equated with a single-minded emphasis on adoption and provide an excuse for continuing to leave on the back-burner these pressing foster care agendas.

References

Department of Health and Social Security (1985) *Social Work Decisions in Child Care*, London: HMSO.

Department of Health (1989) *Patterns and Outcomes in Child Protection*, London: HMSO.

Department of Health (1995) *Looking after Children: Review of Arrangements form*, London: HMSO.

Neil, E. (1999) *Contact After Adoption Newsletter 2*, Norwich: UEA Centre for Research on the Child and Family.

Rutter, M. and the English and Romanian Study Team (1998) 'Developmental catch-up and deficit following adoption after severe global early privation', in *Journal of Child Psychology and Psychiatry*, 39 : 4, pp 465-476.

Sellick, C. and Thoburn, J. (1996) *What works in family placement?*, Barnardo's.

Thoburn, J. (1999) 'Trends in foster care and adoption' in Stevenson, O. (ed) *Child Welfare in the UK, 1948 – 1998*, Oxford: Blackwell Science, pp 121-155.

Utting, W. (1997) *People Like Us: The report of the review of the safeguards for children living away from home*, London: HMSO.

The impact of social work intervention in the preparation and support of late placements

ALAN RUSHTON
Senior Lecturer in
Social Work
Kings College
University of London

The investigation of social work intervention reported here was part of the Maudsley Adoption and Fostering Study and the reader interested in the full details of methods and statistical findings will find them in the main publications from the study (Rushton, Quinton, Dance and Mayes, 1998; and Quinton, Rushton, Dance and Mayes, 1998)). The aim of this part of the research was to describe the extent and nature of social work intervention in late permanent placements and to discover what types and levels of social work support were provided, how they related to the needs of the children and families and what impact the intervention had during the first year of placement.

This research was based on a group of children placed, when aged between five and nine, from care into permanent family placements. It was a prospective design, following 61 boys and girls over the first year of placement. There were 29 girls and 32 boys in the sample and their mean age at placement was 7 years, 5 months (range 59–121 months). Most of the children were white and placed with white families. Of the ten children with at least one parent of minority ethnic origin, half were placed with families who had a similar ethnic background. Information comes from interviews with the new parents, the child's social workers (CSWs) and the family social workers (FSWs) who were all interviewed twice: at one month and 12 months following the new placement.

Preparation of the new parents

Preparation of the new parents was usually undertaken by means of both group and individual sessions. Hearing about the experiences of other foster and adoptive parents was especially popular and found to be the most helpful way to anticipate how life would change once the placement was made.

However, experienced parents were the group most likely to feel critical of the preparation and training they received. It sometimes did not seem to take their particular needs into account and failed to acknowledge their prior parenting experience. The preparation model needed to be re-thought in some cases when it appeared still to be wedded to the methods for the preparation of childless couples. However, many children placed with experienced parents, particularly in families whose birth children were still at home, exhibited more behaviour and relationship problems at the end of the year. This was not explained by more difficult children being placed with established families. It argues for a model of preparation that acknowledges prior parenting experience, but stresses the differences involved in parenting a late placed child, especially for those who have raised children from infancy.

Opportunities are needed for anticipating possible relationship conflicts when other children are present in the home. Parents and professionals should be planning jointly for how these can be effectively addressed.

Adequate preparation should also involve the children living in the new home and helping them to think about the changes that the arrival of a new sibling or siblings will bring. A wide variation was found in the extent to which the birth children of prospective new parents had been prepared or consulted. While some FSWs described extensive initial discussions with birth children, the task was often left for parents to complete.

Organisers of preparation programmes need to remain up to date on research findings concerning the factors most likely to destabilise placements of older children, the common problems experienced by the placed children, the kinds of behaviour new parents find most difficult to handle and the likely impact on family relationships.

Information given about the children before placement

The quality of information given to the new parents about the children to be placed and their backgrounds was poor for a third of the families. The importance of good quality information for new parents has often been stressed. It can help the new parents to understand the children's difficulties in the light of their history and to respond with more understanding to medical, behavioural and educational problems. Possession of information also enabled parents to respond sensitively to the children's questions about their background, especially where there was no contact with the birth family.

New parents are entitled to accurate, comprehensive and up-to-date information. Computerised storage and retrieval systems should be enlisted to speed the bureaucratic process. Although the issue of confidentiality has to be addressed, new parents need the opportunity to discuss in detail and reflect on the experiences of children with whom they are likely to be matched. It was clear that there are occasions when prospective new families do not "hear" all that they are told during the preparation phase. For this reason, the passing on of information should be formally recorded.

In order to gather better quality and more accurate pre-placement information, a multidisciplinary approach to assessment is necessary, augmenting psychological and child psychiatric expertise with social work assessments. Reviews of pre-placement history should pay special attention to factors that have been shown to be predictors of good and poor placement outcome as a means of ensuring that the most relevant information is given prominence.

New parents' stress prior to placement

High levels of stress were experienced by the new parents prior to placement, which were frequently associated with initial meetings with and anticipation of the child or children's arrival. This period of time sharpened the focus dramatically for the intending parents and confronted them with the reality that the child was soon to become part of their daily lives. Some families found the practical demands and the timing of the introductory period made for considerable difficulties. Social workers need to be more aware of the new families' existing commitments when making introductions. This is a taxing period and opportunities need to be given to air anxieties and uncertainties without prejudice, even though they may be quickly forgotten once the child arrives.

Knowledge of factors in the child's background

The study found marked differences in outcome for children who had been singled out and rejected by their birth parent/s. The difficulty these children had in returning affection and expressing feelings created stresses for the new parents. The difficulty of parenting such children has implications for selecting substitute parents, for preparing both the child and the new parents, and for post-placement support. Investigating and selecting the prospective parents could be improved by examining how they might respond to the common behaviours of children who have been rejected, like problems with self-esteem, and their tolerance levels of a child who will take a considerable amount of time to develop warm and trusting relationships.

In relation to work with the children, this finding argues for a thorough assessment of children's experiences in relation to their birth family and for appropriate therapeutic work to be attempted with the child before and during the permanent placement. Both the nature of the rejection and the children's reaction to it should be considered. If the rejection finding is replicated in future studies this will strengthen the guidance to practitioners on which children to target and how to help the new parents. Any encouragement to the parents not to withdraw their affection and to maintain sensitive responses may be helpful in showing the child that the adults are able to withstand the difficult behaviour and will not reject the child as the child may have come to expect from past experience.

Problem levels in the children

The finding that some children's behaviour deteriorates during the first year in spite of placement in a carefully selected home with a plan for permanence is crucial information for prospective parents, for social workers and for policy makers allocating appropriate service levels to these families. The study has provided detailed evidence about the kinds of problems which are common to late placed children. This should enable practitioners to talk to new parents about specific problems like overactive, restless behaviour and non-compliance rather than in global terms like "disturbed" or "damaged".

By the parents' descriptions, the demands on them were often intense. The knowledge of the child's history and current distress were painful to witness and they had a daunting sense of responsibility. Parents were surprised by the strength of their own feelings of pain, anger and frustration. Where there was a lack of someone to talk to, this was felt acutely. Some families wanted simply to "off-load", to have a listening ear and to understand better what they were experiencing. Others wanted something more specific, like help to devise particular strategies to deal with problem behaviour.

Factors in the placement

Placement of children on their own into established families was found to increase the risk of unstable outcomes. Conflict often arose between the incoming child and children already living in the new home. Difficult sibling relationships could develop irrespective of the age gap between the placed child and the birth children. Many of these children had previously experienced rejection and this factor may interact with placement patterns. This finding should give pause for thought to family placement workers who expect experienced families to be better used to dealing with challenging behaviour.

It is important to be aware of any parenting problems as soon as they arise and before negative sequences of interaction become established. This certainly argues for the post placement support workers to know the parents well, to listen carefully to them and to observe interactions. It may be important to employ a dual approach by attempting to modify the child's behaviour, making it easier for parenting to be warmer and more relaxed and by modifying parenting so that the child's behaviour improves.

The development of new relationships

Interest in attachment theory is currently being extended to the process of re-attachment in new relationships. Difficulties in forming mutually satisfying relationships with new parents tended to be linked to an inability to express feelings openly or appropriately, with a perceived lack of trust and lack of genuine affection by the children for their new parents.

Knowledge of how to promote the developing parent–child relationship is still limited. More needs to be known about how flexible the attachment system is and to what extent "internal representations" of adult care givers can be modified with changing experience or with therapeutic intervention. The children who were "slow to attach" frequently taxed the capacity of new parents to maintain their positive feelings. If the new parents are given proper attention in the early stages of placement and the relationship concerns attended to constructively, the other problems the child is exhibiting may be more manageable.

Improving the CSW's practice

It was dispiriting to have to report that much of the child preparation work was under-developed and the aims and methods poorly formulated. Clearly if the work is to be undertaken by mainstream child care workers, they need better training and supervision, proper allocation of time to do the work, and formal legitimation of the task by managers. The recommendations of child care specialists about the importance of preparation of the child do not appear to be finding very full expression in social services departments. Admittedly it is hard to transfer psychological techniques developed in more sequestered clinical environments to these settings and such methods are frequently practised tentatively or in diluted form. Training schemes accrediting social workers to conduct permanent placement work will help to clarify role expectations, set agreed standards for appropriate knowledge and skill, and disseminate expertise. Training should impart better information about child development so that social workers know what to look for in making assessments and planning interventions and they should be encouraged to take a critical look at the developmental model they are using. As more becomes known about appropriate and effective interventions with abused children it will be possible to feed the effective elements into social work training, supervision and practice.

It is of interest that, in the absence of overactive/restless behaviour, a positive association was found between CSW intervention and outcome. The practice implication to be drawn from this finding is that proper psychological assessment of overactivity should be conducted when making choices about the aims and intensity of preparatory work. If the overactivity inhibits the chance of achieving a positive effect, resources may need to be shifted to preparing the new parents specifically to acquire effective techniques for handling this problem. In the earlier follow up study (Rushton, Treseder and Quinton, 1995) overactivity/restlessness remained an enduring problem even eight years after placement.

Some children did receive a high quality preparation service, but they were not necessarily receptive to the help on offer at that point in their lives. It is recognised that abused and neglected children may have difficulty in talking about "internal states" and may have resisted these encounters. If children remain in a state of fear or psychological numbness they may not be able to articulate their needs. It is clearly important to assess how amenable the child is to intensive direct work, to specify the expected benefits and to estimate how long it will take before they may become apparent. These considerations need to be weighed in relation to the time scale of the permanent placement plan and whether the CSW is capable of creating the necessary environment of security and trust to enable the children to resolve their problems.

Direct work with children by field social workers needs a higher profile. This work proved to be highly challenging and complex in many of these cases and skilled supervision and support was often lacking. Structured assessments of the children are needed to understand the origin of their problems, to help decide how much can realistically be achieved and by what means. A considerable gap between theory, practice and research still exists. The assumption in working with abused children is often that losses, trauma and other forms of early adverse experience have to be addressed in order to make progress. However, it may be possible to modify the child's current difficulties which, in so doing, might then reverberate back on the early events and attenuate their continuing effect. Newer methods might be considered which are being adapted for use with children (Reinecke *et al*, 1996) like cognitive therapies and social skills training which stress a more selective approach to intervention, geared to the child's developmental level and using more standardised treatment plans.

No significant associations were found in this study between levels of CSW service and outcome, which was more likely to be explained by prior factors in the child's history. However, this should not necessarily be construed as lack of evidence of effectiveness of the methods themselves, as this was a test of the effect of very heterogeneous social work intervention. It is likely that the broad variations in expertise, the variety of approaches taken and the limited time available reduced the possibility of a large effect on outcome.

Direct work with children, when continued by the child's social worker beyond placement, mostly entailed a completion of interventions started before placement and involved sustained effort to work therapeutically with children who were rejecting, aggressive or slow to attach. Just over half of the new parents reported that they had found the CSW supportive over the course of the year. However, the divided priorities evident in the preparation work of the CSWs continued into placement, and although families understood that demands of child protection work or court appearances had to take precedence, this remained a source of difficulty because of the distress caused to the children by cancelled or postponed appointments.

Another source of discomfort was the conflict between trying to integrate the child into the family on the one hand, while being concerned for the overall supervision of the placement on the other. This was of particular importance in established families, where continued concentration on the placed child could emphasise differences between them and their other children.

The implication for service organisations should not be to remove the CSWs from a task inadequately performed but to recognise the importance and challenge of this work and to identify the skills, training and supervisory support required to sustain it, as well to be realistic about what can be achieved. The best of the CSWs were trying to achieve advanced level work amongst a myriad of other competing and very different demands. An accreditation process should be considered in order to operate quality control of this aspect of the social work service. More specialist training is needed, in particular, courses on behaviour management and on parenting sexually abused children. It is a matter for social services departments to decide whether they want CSWs to provide resource rich services to children.

Improving the FSW's practice

Although FSWs had received more training than CSWs about family placements, through attending day conferences and seminars, surprisingly little training focused specifically on sustaining permanent placements. There is room for a more structured approach to educating social workers about achieving permanence and about the means that are at their disposal for supporting placements. Greater familiarity with research evidence is needed to support assessments and appropriate interventions.

How are the problems the children bring to the placement to be addressed? Simply placing the child in a stable nurturing home does not have the effect of reversing past difficulties. As a first line of help, the social workers supporting the placement should be able to offer effective reassurance and encouragement but also to provide information and to provide, or to recruit, more focused help. They should be competent and confident in advising parents on sensible interventions to reduce the level of difficult behaviour. However, if the problems persist, a referral for more specialist and intensive psychological help may be necessary. This is best managed by a multidisciplinary and multi-agency child mental health team who have familiarised themselves with late placement practice (Hughes, 1995). Such a team will be able to provide a more detailed and comprehensive assessment of the roots of the problems and to offer to work jointly with the family to increase parenting skills and strategies and modify problems like restless and disorganised behaviour.

Despite the considerable recent developments in constructing and evaluating parenting training programmes (Webster-Stratton, 1991), very few published examples exist of the specific application of these methods with substitute parents and late placed children. Kurtz, Thornes and Wolkind (1994) and the Health Advisory Service (1995) have criticised the lack of adequate child and adolescent mental health services for children in local authority care due to poor links, slow referral procedures, long waiting lists and insufficient access to therapeutic services. However, case studies of post adoption intervention are beginning to be published. Examples include intensive work carried out by multidisciplinary teams when placements are in difficulty (Rushton and Rushton, 1996) and a single case study of child psychotherapy with an adopted boy (Lush, Boston, Morgan and Kolvin, 1998). The development of post adoption centres is a welcome innovation in concentrating expertise in this field (Howe, 1990) and links with other parents, hot lines, respite care and support groups should be promoted. The development of appropriate, specialist and accessible resources should help to avoid reliance solely on the FSW service.

References

Howe, D. (1990) 'The Post Adoption Centre: the first three years', in *Adoption & Fostering* 14 : 1, pp 27-31.

Hughes, B. (1995) *Post placement services for children and families: defining the need*, London: Social Services Inspectorate/Department of Health.

Kurtz, Z., Thornes, R. and Wolkind, S. (1994) *Services for the Mental Health of Children and Young People in England: A national review*, London: South Thames RHA.

Lush, D., Boston, M., Morgan, J. and Kolvin, I. (1998) 'Psychoanalytic psychotherapy with disturbed adopted and foster children: a single case follow-up study', in *Journal of Child Psychology and Psychiatry* 3 (1), pp 51-69.

Quinton, D., Rushton, A., Dance, C. and Mayes, D. (1998) *Joining New Families: A study of adoption and fostering in middle childhood*, Chichester: Wiley and Sons.

Reinecke, M., Dattilio, F. and Freeman, A. (eds) (1996) *Cognitive Therapy with Children and Adolescents*, London: The Guilford Press.

Rushton, A., Quinton, D., Dance, C. and Mayes, D. (1998) 'Preparation for permanent placement: evaluating direct work with older children', in *Adoption & Fostering* 21 : 4, pp 41-48.

Rushton, A. and Rushton, A. (1996) 'Adoption and fostering: new perspectives, new research, new practice, in Sigston, A., Curran, P., Labram, A. and Wolfendale, S. (eds) *Psychology in Practice with Young People, Families and Schools*, London: David Fulton Publishers.

Rushton, A., Treseder, J. and Quinton, D. (1995) 'An 8 year prospective study of older boys placed in permanent substitute families', in *Journal of Child Psychology and Psychiatry*, 36 : 4, pp 687-695.

Webster-Stratton, C. (1991) 'Annotation: strategies for helping families with conduct disordered children', in *Journal of Child Psychology and Psychiatry*, 32, pp 1047-1062.

The use of story stem narratives in assessing the inner world of the child: Implications for adoptive placements

MIRIAM STEELE
University College,
London
Anna Freud Centre

JILL HODGES
Great Ormond Street
Hospital

JEANNE KANIUK
Thomas Coram
Adoption Service

KAY HENDERSON
University College
London

SAUL HILLMAN
Anna Freud Centre

PAUL BENNETT
Anna Freud Centre

Introduction

This report[1] is intended as a brief overview of an ongoing research project which is aiming to apply recent advances in developmental psychological research – and specifically in the field of attachment research – to an area of important clinical relevance, the area of child maltreatment, foster care and adoptive placements. By applying new techniques to both the evaluation of adults[2] who are wishing to become adoptive parents and to assessment of the "hard to place" child, prior to placement and following through into the first two years post placement, we hope to refine the capacity to "fit" particular parents to a particular child's needs. We also aim to provide a picture of the child's internal world especially with regard to their initial perceptions and expectations of parent–child relationships which will help new adoptive parents and professionals in their understanding and management of the child's behaviour. The specific focus of this report is the method we are applying to assess children's inner working models of attachment: story stem narratives.

We are attempting to assess the children's representational worlds by video and audio-recording their verbal and non-verbal responses to an interviewer's presentation of a series of family conflicts with the help of doll figures where children are asked to 'show me and tell me what happens next'. This technique has been previously used and validated as a measure of attachment processes in preschool and school-aged children from both non-clinical and clinical samples (e.g.Bretherton, Ridgeway and Cassidy, 1990; Buchsbaum and Emde, 1990; Buchsbaum *et al.*, 1992). The MacArthur Network of researchers including leading developmental psychologists (e.g. Inge Bretherton) and psychoanalysts (e.g. Robert Emde) pioneered the recent and growing interest in studying children's narratives. Their investigations suggest that the emotional themes in children's responses tend to remain more-or-less stable in normative circumstances between three and five years of age (Oppenheim, Emde and Warren, 1997). Further, the emotional integration or lack of such organisation in children's responses appears to be indicative of the absence or presence of behaviour problems according to parental reports (Warren, Oppenheim, and Emde, 1996).

The specific interest in collecting story-stem completions in this study is for their potential to provide access to meaning children have derived from their experiences of troubled and painful attachment histories, prior to placement. While these histories may be expected to provide the child's initial model for perceiving new parental figures, and thus exert a powerful influence on the developing relationship, a number of questions remain

---

1. The study is funded by the Tedworth and Glasshouse Trust from the Sainsbury Trusts.
2. For a brief elaboration on the method we are employing to assess adoptive parents' inner worlds, namely the Adult Attachment Interview, see Steele, Kaniuk, Hodges, Haworth & Huss, in this volume.

concerning this social-emotional baggage carried by the child into his or her adoptive placement. Specifically, what is the child carrying into the new adoptive relationship? To what extent may the story-stem completions collected at the time of placement reveal evidence of the integration of prior maltreatment or the probable experience of one or more benign or compensatory attachments prior to placement? And when the story-stem completions are collected some considerable time after adoptive placement, to what extent will they reveal that the new attachment relationship has becomes a positive transmuting influence upon the child's inner world and social relations? To investigate these issues, the longitudinal investigation – on which the present report is based – is administering the story-completion task both at the time of adoptive placement and again one and two years later. This will allow the examination of the possibility of changes in children's perceptions, expectations and feelings about attachment relationships as they begin, hopefully, to experience more benign parent–child interactions than were available to them previously.

Data from the first phase of this longitudinal investigation is included in this report which is based on a cross-sectional comparison among four groups in order to explore the potentially very different range of story-stem completions provided by:

- a recently adopted group of "hard-to-place" children participating in the first phase of the longitudinal study described above;

- a residential clinical comparison group of children from similarly harsh and adverse backgrounds not yet in a permanent adoptive placement;

- a comparison group of children matched in terms of economic background and predominantly single-parent status but children who are not (yet) on at-risk registers; and

- a middle-class comparison group from intact families.

Method

The narrative stems method
This technique of assessment addresses aspects of children's mental representations of self, others, and relationships, based on their experience of their attachment history. It allows the child's attachment representations to be evidenced in a displaced way, which is usually enjoyed by the child and not experienced as unduly threatening. The battery of story stems that are being used in this study derive from two sources. The first five story stems are ones that were originally developed by Jill Hodges (Hodges, 1992) in the context of her work with the Child Care Consultation team at the Hospital for Sick Children at Great Ormond Street. All of these stories are designed to evoke material from clinically referred children concerning their thoughts and feelings in relation to attachment constructs, such as the degree to which the child represents adults as comforting and capable of caregiving as compared to injuring or neglectful. Two of the five stories are depicted with the use of animal figures, which enable the child to engage in the stories at a somewhat more manageable distance from those that only include human doll figures. A further eight stories are being used in the study which have been selected from a larger battery of 14 stories that

originate with the MacArthur Foundation Network on Childhood narratives headed by Professor Robert Emde. These stories cover a range of dilemmas deemed pertinent to children between four and eight years of age.

The method uses a standard series of narrative stems – brief semi-structured play situations. The adult begins the story, telling it in words and simultaneously showing it with small doll and animal figures, and then invites the child to 'show me and tell me what happens next'. Thus, importantly, both verbal and nonverbal modes of communication are available to the child. The stories include the following domestic dilemmas:

- a child spilling juice at the dinner table;

- a mother asking for the television to be turned off as she has a headache followed by the child's best friend arriving at the door demanding that the friends watch their favourite television show;

- a mother urging her impatient child to wait while she prepares dinner with the eventual consequence that the child reaches for the stove and ends up with a burnt hand; and

- an explicitly moral dilemma involving a child who has been instructed by mother (slipping next door for a moment) 'not to touch anything on the bathroom shelf' after which the child's sibling cuts a finger.

We assure the families who are participating in the study that the children will never be asked directly to speak about their difficult histories.

The interviews are videotaped and transcribed. The transcript covers both speech and the child's non-verbal narrative as shown with the dolls and animals. Ratings of attachment-related representations are then made according to a manual of criteria (Hodges, Steele, Henderson, and Hillman, 1998). For instance, children's responses are rated for the appearance of themes which convey parents/adults viewed as sources of comfort, as protective, as frightening, as unconcerned; the manual also includes codes for representation of the various figures as injured or dead. The responses to the narratives are also rated for stories which convey bizarre elements or ones that can be considered "catastrophic fantasies" which have been noted in the literature as highly indicative of disorganised/controlling children likely to have experienced trauma or likely to have been parented by caregivers unresolved with respect to past trauma or loss (Main, 1995). The way in which the child approaches the task are covered by ratings of disengagement or changing the constraints in the stories which accounts for the child not being able to address themselves to the particular conflict presented in the story stem.

The samples

We have been collecting story stem narratives from a variety of sources in order to gather data that will help compare the content and mode of expression from children with a range of histories and current environments. The four groups comprising of children between the ages of four and seven years, have been collected from the following sources:

1. Thomas Coram Adopted Group

This group comprises of 16 children who have recently been placed by the Thomas Coram Adoption Service. They are comparable to the Clinical group in terms of the presence of adverse histories but have now been placed with new adoptive parents.

2. Clinical Group

The data that forms this group of 26 children originates from two sources. The first are children who have been brought to Department of Psychological Medicine at Great Ormond Street for a specialist assessment by the Childcare Consultation Team. The second source comes from children currently residing at the Caldecott Community, a therapeutic children's home. The children in this group had similar features of adverse family experiences ranging from family dysfunction to extreme abuse.

3. Matched Group

This group comprises of 30 children who have been matched for age and demographic variables (SES, lone parent families) but have not come to the authority's attention for issues of the quality of care in the family.

4. The London Parent Child Project

The data for this group is derived from a cohort of 90 first born children who have been participating in a longitudinal study of attachment relationships since just prior to their birth (Steele, Steele and Fonagy, 1996). They have been followed at 12 months, 18 months, five and six years. The story stem narratives that were coded using the Hodges *et al* system were collected at the five year visit. These children comprise a rather homogenous group from predominantly middle class two parent families.

Example of a story-stem narrative

The following are two examples from children's responses to one of the MacArthur story stems. The "burnt hand" stem presents the child with the alarming circumstance of a child's hand being burned on account of his inability to inhibit his impulses (hunger) at the request of mother. Will the hurt hand be tended to? If so, by whom? And, given that the child was hungry for dinner, and mother was ostensibly trying to meet this need, will dinner be served? To whom? By whom? The story is told to the child as follows.

Example from Adopted Group

Lyle spent the first six years of his life in and out of foster care placements having been removed from the care of his biological mother because of what was judged to be her inability to care for Lyle and his three-year-old brother. Mother was described as "strung out" on drugs much of the time such that Lyle was indeed often responsible for caring for himself, his brother and his mother in the face of an ever-changing background of boyfriends. There was evidence of physical abuse and neglect. His behaviour at home with his new adoptive parents was described as provocative, aggressive, and cruel in relation to his younger brother with alternating compliant and wishing to please behaviour. He was also, however, described as sociable and an "expert player".

Lyle (aged seven) responds below to the "burnt hand" stem:

Lyle's response to the burnt hand story

L: He washed it and then he ate it up and he said I want to play in the paddling pool and Daddy came in soaking wet saying, 'Where's my dinner! Where's my dinner! Where, where, where's my dinner?' And then he jumped onto the cooker and he poked his head in there and then he was so strong he picked the cooker up (shows doll balancing cooker in the air). And then he goes to the cooker and says this makes a nice house.

Comment: L begins by indicating that there is no adult available to help minister to the burnt hand, the boy ministers to his own needs. With seeming omnipotence, he washes his hand and eats up his supper from the hot pan, presumably lying on the floor. Then a still more ominous figure emerges in the story, an ogre-like figure who is father. Father's demandingness and power leads him 'to jump into the cooker' before demonstrating his strength by picking the cooker up. The bizarre image of father in the cooker is carried forward into father declaring the cooker makes a nice house. The (re)presentation of father is fiery, fearful and bizarre.

M: What about George's burnt hand?

L: He washed it and wraps it in a plaster.

Comment: L reiterates the theme of self-reliance. This boy takes care of himself as it seems that he has learned to cope by allowing only himself to minister to his needs.

M: Does his Mum say anything about his hurt hand?

L: No, but then George says, 'I'll cook the dinner! Dinner is served!' But then (L makes loud munching noises) the little brother scoffed the lot, leaving just a titchy bit. Only for a rat to eat. One crumb of it, cuz it was steak and kidney pie, leaving just crumbs of it.

Comment: L. continues with his theme of the self as all-powerful, taking over the role of provider for himself and, spontaneously introduced into the narrative, the younger brother who devours all the goodies.

L: (Takes little brother doll and has Mother doll say) 'You are tired' (little boy doll says) 'No, I'm not.' Mother says, 'Yes, you are and I know that. Now you naughty little rascal you need a good sleep, go to your bed without your supper.' (L has little boy doll say in very babyish voice) 'I want my mother, I want my mother'. Mother doll says, 'Go to bed till the morning, you little rascal'. (L drags boy doll to behind cooker.)

Comment: L. reveals something more about his (re)presentation of mother, i.e. she can be a disciplinarian who sends the little brother to bed without his supper demeaning him only slightly with terms which depict anger but also endearment, e.g. 'You little rascal'.

L: Then the boy jumps on the cooker and says, 'Where's my breakfast?' and the Mum says, 'You get in the frying pan' and he says, 'Good, we've got a nice meal' and puts him on the stove and he cooked roast brother!

Comment: The (re)presentation of mother takes on a harsh and punitive/maltreating form when, at mother's initiative, she and George cook little brother.

Example from London Parent Child Project

M: Mum says to Susan, 'We're going to have a good supper but it's not ready yet. Don't get too close to the stove.'
Susan says, 'That looks good. I don't want to wait. I'd like some now.'
Susan knocks the pan off the stove. 'Ow, I've burnt my hand! It hurts!'
'Show me and tell me what happens next?'

(C indicates child, I indicates interviewer)

C: Oh, poor you, you should be careful. Oh, come sit on my lap.

I: Mum says, 'Be careful', so what else happens?

C: She sits on mummy's lap.

I: She sits on mummy's lap.

C: She sits on mummy's lap cuz she hurt herself and she stays there for a long time. Then one of the brothers comes in and asks what's wrong with Susan and Susan says what happens and the brother says he is hungry too. Then Mum says everybody needs to wait and now she can't cook the dinners they will have to wait even longer.

The narrative this little girl gives in response to the stem is characterised by a brief, matter-of-fact style that addresses the main conflict presented in the stem. This child's first comment is that the little girl doll figure is comforted by an adult doll figure both verbally and physically. The obvious hurt in the story is acknowledged in an explicit way leading to an inference that the child has a representation of adults as being able to offer comfort and care. The story them moves on to include other members of the family in what feels like a typical scenario. The narrative is coherent in that the elaborations she makes are easy to comprehend and she offers a reasonable ending to the story.

Results

The statistical results presented below comprise of a sampling from the preliminary analyses comparing the coding of story stem narratives of the four groups.

Acknowledgement of Distress (See Chart 1)
This code is rated when a child shows that one of the figures portrayed in the story provided by the interviewer has registered distress. An example of a narrative where a child received a positive rating on this code would be where they narrate, 'he's crying', in response to the distress one of the characters felt when lost.

The results show that the children from the London Parent Child Project were more likely to include this theme in the content of their stories as compared to the other three groups. The Coram Adopted group and the Matched comparison group showed these themes significantly less often than the London Parent Child Project group but more often than the children in the Clinical group. It may be that being placed in a new adoptive home has enabled the children to begin to shift from a more defensive stance of denying distress as is evidence by the children in the clinical groups.

Chart 1
Acknowledgement of Distress Mean Aggregate Ratings

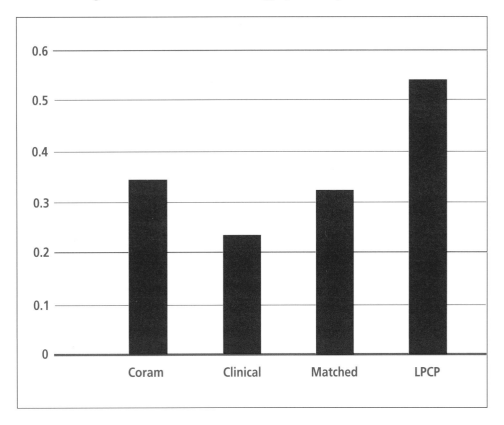

Adult/Injured Dead (See Chart 2)
This code indicated if the child presents either verbally or in play that one of the figures deemed to represent an adult was in either an injured or dead state. Here we see that this was a theme presented relatively infrequently by the London Parent Child Project children as compared to the other three groups. The children comprising the Clinical group included this theme most and the Coram Adopted and Matched comparison children showed indications of this theme to a moderate degree. In terms of the theoretical underpinnings of the study in terms of attachment theory, it would seem that the children in the highest risk groups do not possess a representation of adults as being in a position to maintain a parental role if they are depicted as injured or dead.

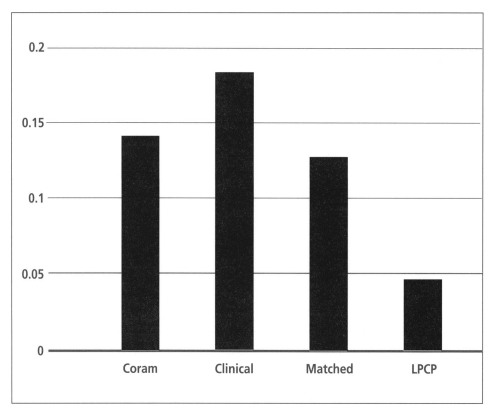

Chart 2
Adult Injured/Dead Mean Aggregate Ratings

Sibling/Peer Helps (See Chart 3)
This code is rated if the child's narrative includes a reference to a figure deemed to represent a child as being helpful in relation to the conflict presented. Interestingly we see that the Matched comparison group present this theme more often than any of the other groups, including the London Parent Child Project children. This is understood to be linked to the possibility that siblings and peers may play a more important supportive role in the Clinical, Matched and newly Adopted Coram group as compared to the children in the London Parent Child Project cohort who are all first born children and have a lower risk status than the children in the other three groups.

Disengagement (See Chart 4)
Narrative responses are coded with Disengagement if a child begins to give a narrative and then breaks off engaging with the story telling process so that the process is not completed. Interestingly, we see here that it is the Coram Adopted group that is scored most often on this code in comparison with the other three groups. This may be an indication of the increased anxiety in being assessed early on in a new placement. The London Parent Child Project children were rarely rated on this code as they were able to engage in the task readily.

Chart 3
Sibling/Peer Helps Mean Aggregate Ratings

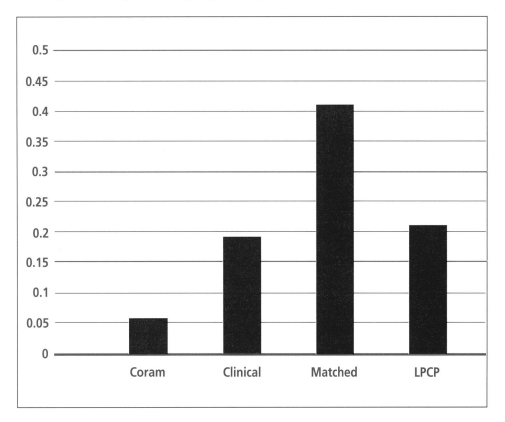

Chart 4
Disengagement Mean Aggregate Ratings

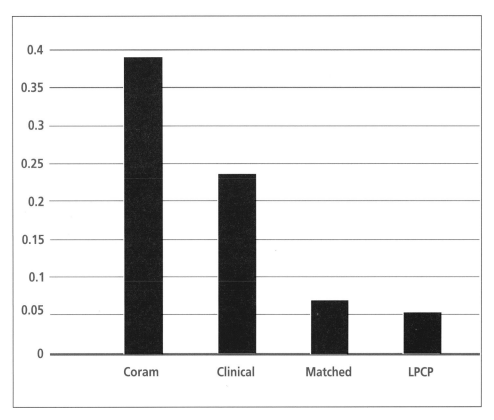

Discussion

The results reported here underline the value of story stem (and doll-figure) narrative techniques for investigating children's inner (mental) representations of self and others – the domain of attachment theorising. Importantly, the present results confirm that fantasies involving injury and/or death to adults are extremely rare in the "normal" population of middle-class children living in intact families; by contrast, such aggressive themes are highly common in children living in circumstances where the child may have experienced directly or indirectly injury or harm perpetrated by an adult. While it is not the case that one can directly make an isomorphic link between the responses children give to the story stems, their mental representations and actual experiences, by comparing the narratives from children whose experiences have differed we are able to infer something of the way in which the external environment facilitates or impinges upon the children's inner world. Importantly, we can infer that the data presented here are coded from responses given by children in their own voice, using their own words and in their own narrative form. This method of data collection contrasts with the more routinely used parental self report measures which may constrain our capacities to harvest a more telling window into the child's experiences and the way that these are integrated into their cognitive, social and emotional development. Careful study of the child's narrative often provides very vivid illustrations of aspects of a child's attachment representations, and also reflects some of the defences and coping mechanisms children use to handle experiences of distress, which may suggest their likely response in a new family context.

References

Bretherton, I., Ridgeway, D., and Cassidy, J. (1990) 'Assessing internal working models of the attachment relationship: an attachment story completion task for 3-year-olds', in Greenberg, M. T., Cicchetti, D. and Cummings, E. M. (eds) *Attachment in the Preschool Years: Theory, research and intervention* (pp 273-308), Chicago: University of Chicago Press.

Buchsbaum, H. K. and Emde, R. N. (1990) 'Play narratives in 36-month-old-children: early moral development and family relationships', in *Psychoanalytic Study of the Child* 40, pp 129-155.

Buchsbaum, H. K., Toth, S. L., Clyman, R. B., Cicchetti, D. and Emde, R. N. (1992) 'The use of a narrative story-stem technique with maltreated children: implications for theory and practice', in *Development and Psychopathology* 4, pp 603-625.

George, C., Kaplan, N. and Main, M. (1985) *The Adult Attachment Interview*, unpublished manuscript, Berkeley: University of California.

Main, M., Kaplan, N. and Cassidy, J. (1985) 'Security in infancy, childhood and adulthood: A move to the level of representation', in Bretherton, I. and Waters, E. (eds) *Growing Points in Attachment Theory and Research* (pp 66-104), Monographs of the Society for Research in Child Development 50, Serial No. 209.

Hodges, J. (1992) *Little Piggy Story Stem Battery*, unpublished manuscript.

Hodges, J., Steele, M., Henderson, K. and Hillman S. (1998) *Coding Manual for Story Stem Narrative Responses*, unpublished manuscript.

Main, M. (1995) 'Recent studies in attachment: overview, with selected implication for clinical work', in Goldberg, S., Muir, R. and Kerr, J. (eds) *Attachment Theory: Social development and clinical perspectives*, Hillsdale, NJ: Analytic Press.

Oppenheim, D., Emde, R. and Warren, S. (1997) 'Children's narrative representations of mothers: their development and associations with child and mother adaptation', in *Child Development*, 68, pp 127-138.

Steele, H., Steele, M. and Fonagy, P. (1996) 'Associations among attachment classifications of mothers, fathers, and their infants', in *Child Development*, 67, pp 541-556.

Warren, S., Oppenheim, D. and Emde, R. (1996) 'Can emotions and themes in children's play predict behaviour problems?', in *Journal of the American Academy of Child and Adolescent Psychiatry*, 34, pp 1331-1337.

The use of the Adult Attachment Interview: Implications for assessment in adoption and foster care

MIRIAM STEELE
University College
London
Anna Freud Centre
JEANNE KANIUK
Thomas Coram
Adoption Service
JILL HODGES
Great Ormond Street
Hospital
CINDY HAWORTH
Anna Freud Centre
SHAUN HUSS
Anna Freud Centre

Introduction

This report* stems from an ongoing research project which is aiming to apply recent advances in developmental psychological research – and specifically in the field of attachment research – to the area of foster care and adoptive placements. Specifically, this report concentrates upon the results obtained from administering the Adult Attachment Interview (AAI) to a selected group of parents who successfully adopted developmentally delayed children. These parents were also interviewed concerning their experience of the adoption and the results below will include a comparison of the responses to both interviews. Notably, while the AAI has been widely used in mainstream developmental research of parent–child relationships, the interview has not so far been extended to studies of parent–child pairs founded on an adoptive rather than biological basis, nor to the case of parents who take on the challenge of adopting a disabled child. Thus, the aim of the present investigation was to meet this need for applying the AAI to the task of better understanding the thoughts and feelings concerning attachment among a group of adoptive parents who, according to social work reports and other measures, have developed a positive parent–child relationship and facilitated developmental progress in their adoptive disabled children.

Background

The theoretical framework we rely on for understanding parent–child relationships is the one advanced by John Bowlby (1951; 1979; 1988) and Mary Ainsworth (e.g. Ainsworth, Blehar, Waters, and Wall, 1978), the architects of attachment theory and research. While Bowlby's theoretical formulations broadened our view of the importance of early experience on later development, it was Mary Ainsworth's work which made possible the empirical investigation of attachment theory by identifying distinctive secure and insecure patterns of infant–parent attachment observable in 12–18 month-old children upon their reunion with the parent following two brief separations from the parent. Attachment security during early childhood is denoted by a capacity to express negative feelings and behaviours upon separation from a parent and even more importantly to settle and return to often joyful play and exploration during the reunion with parents; in other words, to use the parent as a secure base. Attachment insecurity during early childhood is observable when a child is either avoidant or resistant (inconsolable) upon reunion following a separation. These patterns are considered to be organised strategies, developed in response to actual caregiving behaviour over time. These interactions impact on the child and provoke a habitual style of responding to the relationship which either dampens their own displays of emotion in the avoidant classifications or heightens the emotional displays in the resistant patterns. Both of these are

* The study is funded by the Tedworth and Glasshouse Trust from the Sainsbury Trusts.

seen to function as useful albeit defensive strategies, which shield the individual from pain in the case of the avoidant strategy or are attempts to draw the caregiver near as in the resistant category.

Most ominously, and only recently recognised as the spotlight of developmental investigations have turned to clinical populations, is the young child who shows obvious signs of fear in the presence of the parent. This fear suggests that the child has been frequently directly or indirectly frightened by the parent's behaviour (Main, 1990). Since the 1970s and ongoing, these secure, insecure and fearful (or disorganised) infant patterns of behaviour have been examined in the context of a number of longitudinal studies of child and parent development spanning linguistic and cultural boundaries (e.g. Sroufe, 1988; Grossmann and Grossman, 1991; Main, Kaplan, and Cassidy, 1985). Notably, these studies have in recent years pointed to distinctive patterns of parental attachment which appear to be the antecedents to previously observed infant patterns of attachment. The suggestion of such a causal link emerges from an observed overlap between infant patterns of attachment assessed by pre-verbal behavioural methods in infancy (in the Strange Situation) and adult/parental patterns of attachment assessed by the detailed study of speech patterns relied upon by adults when discussing the quality and meaning of their attachment experiences. Mary Main, a student of Ainsworth's, heralded the important new phase to attachment research by formulating the corollary measure to the robust Strange Situation to be used with adults, the Adult Attachment Interview.

Methodology

The Adult Attachment Interview

The adult patterns of attachment refer to different strategies adults rely on when faced with the task of making sense of their childhood relations with parents or caregivers, as is demanded by the questions comprising the Adult Attachment Interview (AAI). The signal feature of the autonomous strategy is coherence and a strong valuing of attachment. While the dismissing and preoccupied patterns each represent different forms of incoherence arising out of negative attachment experiences that appear not to have been integrated evenly into the adult's sense of self. The dismissing strategy leads to global evaluations of a good or normal childhood that cannot be supported by relevant memories. The preoccupied strategy leads to global evaluations of a difficult childhood that are accompanied by an overabundance of memories from childhood and adulthood that lead the speaker into feelings of current anger or a sense of resignation to difficulties that cannot be overcome. Finally, the unresolved pattern which may be present in an otherwise dismissing, preoccupied or autonomous interview is applied when an adult shows signs of ongoing grief and disorientation concerning some past loss or trauma. Further, these strategies or patterns operate outside of awareness, playing a significant role in determining the speech an adult uses to answer the questions – questions designed to 'surprise the unconscious' (George, Kaplan and Main, 1985).

The Adult Attachment Interview is structured entirely around the topic of attachment, principally the individual's relationship to their mother and father (and/or to alternative caregivers) during childhood. Interviewees are asked both to describe their relationship with their parents during childhood and to provide specific memories to support global evaluations. The interviewer asks directly about childhood experiences of rejection, being upset, ill and hurt as well as loss, abuse and separations. In addition, the subject is asked to offer explanations for the parents' behaviour and to describe the current relationship with their parents and the influence they consider their childhood experiences to have had upon their adult personality.

Ultimate classification of the interview into the secure or one of the insecure groups depends largely on the extent to which the narrative is judged to satisfy four criteria of coherence:

- a good fit between memories and evaluations concerning attachment;

- a succinct yet complete picture;

- the provision of relevant details;

- clarity and orderliness (Main and Goldwyn, in press).

The basic classification system assigns interviews to one of three groups, two insecure and one secure:

- insecure–dismissing, an interview which is brief but incomplete, marked by a lack of fit between memories and evaluations;

- insecure–preoccupied, an interview which is neither succinct nor complete and contains many irrelevant details, together with much passive speech or high current anger; and

- autonomous–secure, an interview which robustly fulfils all or most of the criteria of coherence.

In addition, alongside the best-fitting classification, some interviews are also considered unresolved with respect to past trauma or loss. An interview is considered unresolved when the speaker refers to loss or trauma in a way that suggests an extreme bereavement reaction, and/or lapses in the monitoring of speech concerning the loss or trauma which, for example, suggest that the speaker harbours irrational feelings of guilt, or an irrational belief that a dead relative is actually alive. Criteria for deciding whether or not an interview is unresolved, and secure versus insecure, together with a set of 30 interval-rating scales (including one for lack of resolution of mourning) comprise the Manual for Rating and Classifying AAIs (Main and Goldwyn, in press). Training in the use of this 200 page document involves attendance at a two-week training session (taught by Mary Main or one of her designated "trainers") which is followed by extensive tests of inter-rater agreement.

The Adult Attachment Interviews in this study were conducted and transcribed verbatim by two social workers, Cindy Haworth and Shaun Huss, who collected the data in partial fulfilment of their M.Sc. degree. Miriam Steele who was "blind" to any identifying features of the participants rated the AAIs.

Experience of Adoption Interview

The interview questions concerning adoption were put to respondent parents, immediately following the Adult Attachment Interview. The Experience of Adoption Interview consists of queries aimed at eliciting a narrative surrounding the adult's reasons for adopting in general, and a disabled child in particular, as well as issues concerning their thoughts and feelings regarding the past, present and future status of the child. Central to the Experience of Adoption Interview protocol was the aim of gaining an account of the parent's initial feelings upon meeting the adopted child. Correspondingly, the interview aimed to yield an estimate of how long it took to establish an enduring sense of joy at being with the child – what Bowlby (1951) had described as the crucial ingredient to a healthy parent–child relationship.

The sample

The Thomas Coram Adoption Service highlighted 30 individuals who had adopted children who suffered from some form of developmental disability and who they considered to have benefited from "successful" placements. The disabilities ranged in severity and included children with Down's Syndrome, hearing and/or sight impairment, and severe developmental delays. Success in this context refers to the fact that the adoption had not broken down, and the children were observed to be moving along developmental milestones within the range of their potential. From this original group, 25 individuals agreed and participated in the study. The mean age of the participants was 46 years. In terms of education and income level, 68 per cent of the sample were in a middle-income bracket and 48 per cent had completed a university degree. The nature of the disability also varied widely from moderate physical disabilities to extremely challenging behavioural problems and learning disabilities, with most falling in a "moderate" category. None of these demographic features were associated with the main interview-based findings of the study summarised below.

Summary of findings

The results will be presented in three sections:

● Adult Attachment Interview results;

● Experience of Adoption Interview; and

● Comparison of the AAI results with data from the Experience of Adoption Interview.

1. Adult Attachment Interview results

In terms of the distribution of attachment classification assigned to the interview transcripts, 32% (n=8) were assigned to the autonomous group, 52% (n=14) to the dismissing group and 16% (n=4) were assigned to the pre-occupied group. These distributions are somewhat skewed from what has been reported in the wider population, where approximately 70% are usually classified as autonomous and 20% are rated as dismissing, with a further 10% classified as pre-occupied.

While many of the interviews did not fulfil the criteria to be classified as Autonomous–Secure on the Adult Attachment Interview Rating Scale (Main &

Goldwyn, in press), they did convey a sense of resilience in the face of adversities either faced in the past or present. These adults seem particularly able to face challenges with optimism and fervour which is of obvious benefit to the children they adopted.

A noteworthy distinguishing feature to this particular sample's attachment interview was the high frequency of experiences of loss, where 96% reported having endured a loss of someone close to them during childhood or adulthood (e.g. parent, spouse, sibling, child). Importantly, when looked at in detail, a remarkable figure concerning apparent resilience stands out: despite the inflated number of individuals who suffered from loss experiences only three interviews were rated as indicative of chronic grief or lack of resolution of mourning with regard to the loss.

The following excerpt conveys an example of the hallmark of the autonomous interview in which the individual describes a loving relationship with mother during her childhood. This mother also expressed a high degree of insight and capacity to reflect upon her own childhood history when she described her relationship with her own mother as involving 'listening and talking'. When asked to elaborate she said, 'Yeah, I think – it's probably the major thing that um both my parents taught me – really is that, um, they listened but sometimes not just to listen to what I was actually saying but what I wasn't saying as well'.

On the other hand, there were a number of interviews that were characterised by descriptions of their childhoods which indicated a sense of lacking in a loving relationship. For example, one parent in response to the question on the Adult Attachment interview 'When you were upset as a child what would you do?' gave the following response: 'Not very much, if I got upset, I wouldn't run to anybody and cry because we didn't do that, I can't remember – I know many many many years later when I was with my dad and I talked properly for the first time, um, I can remember then – a cuddle but I don't think he ever cuddled when I was child and I don't actually think my mom did either but she must have done – but I can't remember feeling upset. Maybe I just didn't get upset very often.' This particular example comes from an interview that was not rated as autonomous but instead as dismissing. The overall narrative suggested a strong effort to minimise the influence of childhood difficulties upon present functioning. A central organising feature of these interviews judged dismissing which characterised approximately half the sample was the pride they conveyed in the speaker's sense of personal strength and distance from troubling emotions. It would seem that this stance toward close relationships might inform an optimistic frame of mind that would be of tremendous benefit when dealing with the day-to-day care of a child with special needs. Turning away from past relationship difficulties was associated in many respondents' interviews to a close attention to the fine details of their adoptive children's capacities and development. The final questions of the Adult Attachment Interview which ask respondents to consider their wishes for the future of their child(ren) elicited many illustrations of a capacity to see small increments in developmental progress as uniquely momentous, which would obviously be of great benefit to the disabled child and the likelihood of further forward moves.

It is important to point out that the system for rating and classifying Adult Attachment Interviews allows for the possibility of reliably identifying individuals who have endured less than favourable childhood experiences with caregivers but who are unlikely to repeat these patterns with their own children. Consider the following example from an interview judged autonomous (a label which usefully underlines the healthy adjustment an adult may achieve despite involving painful attachment experiences during childhood): This individual gave "distant" as one of his adjectives to describe his father. When asked to elaborate, he provided the following description, 'Distant, yeah, um – I suppose overall I didn't feel close to him um... I'm trying to think – it's these sorts of overall impressions and feelings of childhood. I mean he wasn't around on the same level. He wasn't approachable in the same way. He didn't put me to bed and read me bedtime stories. The time he did spend with me was the exception rather than the rule.' In this brief excerpt and elsewhere in the interview, the speaker conveys a sense of having gained a clear understanding of how a parent should invest emotionally in a relationship with his child, though clearly this was gained despite, not because of, his own early experience.

2. Experience of Adoption Interview

The participants were asked a series of questions regarding their experience of the adoption. These ranged from a general question as to their motivation to adopt, to more specific questions about their thoughts about their child with special needs. Perhaps the most common shared feature of these interviews was the fact that 80% of these were adults who specifically sought to adopt a child with special needs (and would not have considered adopting a child without special needs). Relatedly, the interviews indicated that 64% (87% of women and 44% of the men) had prior experience with disability either through personal experiences with family members or friends. In fact, 80% of the women worked in a human services profession such as social work, nursing, physical therapy or institutions of care for disabled individuals. This prior and ongoing experience is perhaps linked to the spontaneous remarks made by many of the respondents (50%) who spoke of their unique ability to cope with the task of parenting a child with special needs. They cited their particular capacity for loving these children as the antecedent to their capacity to cope with the additional demands that were made.

Another feature in these interviews was the ability to speak about a wide range of feelings that were provoked by the relationships with their children. One parent remarked, 'She's an angel and a devil'. Another said, 'She is a gorgeous pain in the neck, fun to have around'. Another said, 'Some days you love him to bits, other days you want to send him to the other part of the world'. One parent clearly regarded the range of emotions experienced as 'she's done things with my emotions no one else has, she brings me from complete and utter happiness to the depths of despair in half an hour'. Many parents made intensely positive descriptions of their child: 'he's the best thing since sliced bread', 'absolutely wonderful', 'perfect, beautiful, clever', 'and bubbly, lively with lots of love'.

3. Comparison of AAI ratings with Experience of Adoption Interview

There was a significant correlation between mother's views of their children in the future as being more independent than dependent and ratings on the

AAI such as loving mother (p>.01) and loving father (p=<.05) This suggests that having experienced one's own parents as nurturing allows the adoptive parent to have in mind goals for their disabled child which include autonomous functioning which may in turn facilitate the functioning of such a child. For example, one parent whose transcript was classified as autonomous in the AAI and responded to a question about her hopes for what the future might hold for their child said, 'I hope that he will gain some independence for his life – um not because I won't be prepared to care for him for the rest of my life but because I think that he's capable of it and that he deserves to have some quality in his life that he can get on – so I would wish for him to have a degree of independence whether in living arrangements or working or whatever.'

Some parents whose interviews were classified as dismissing were nonetheless able to convey a valuing of the relationship with their child despite a less than optimal relationship described with their own parents. For example, in relation to a question about their experience of the adoption one said, 'Pretty much harder than I realised, if I'm really being honest. I should have realised that, with all the things that she'd been through in early childhood. I mean she was quite deprived, really a lot. But you can only go so far. Things have been a lot tougher than I realised or wanted to realise but she's given lots of love, and I wouldn't put the clock back again. It is hard emotionally and mentally, but she's also given much more in terms of love and fun than I could have possibly imagined.'

Implications of the study

The sample of 25 parents studied confirms the observation of Macaskill (1985) that individuals who select to adopt a child with special needs appear to carry within them backgrounds involving adversity. The present results confirm and extend this earlier observation by pointing out how these challenges to well-being appear to have been coped with by utilising diverse strategies, which can be identified from transcripts obtained in response to the AAI. While the sample is really too small to draw strong conclusions, it can highlight the interplay between representations of significant relationships in childhood and the subsequent capacity to provide a background of safety and positive parenting to a special group of children who most undeniably benefit from the match.

Further research involving the use of the AAI with larger numbers of parents who are being selected for the onerous task of caregiving children who are "hard to place" for a variety of reasons might further illuminate the characteristics in adults which make them particularly well suited to take on the responsibilities involved. The social workers who approved these applications to adopt were obviously similarly impressed by this 'resilient-characteristic' of these adults, and their positive decision to support the adult's wish to become an adoptive parent is in part based on this consideration. Notably, the length of time taken by a social worker to build up a profile of an applicant to adopt takes many weeks, multiple interviews and home observations which obviously cover much of the same ground that the AAI does, but perhaps not quite in the same structured way that would allow for the analysis of the information as outlined by the Main rating system. The interview could usefully be included on occasion, as part of the social work agency's battery of assessment tools, one which has an impressive track record in terms of its reliable ability to detect parenting difficulties rooted in painful past experiences.

From the perspective of developmental science, research of the kind presented here permits one to investigate the formation and maintenance of attachment relationships between parents and children where a biological connection is not the starting point. Such data are crucial to the scientific interest in isolating the processes involved in the social transmission of attachment across generations.

References

Ainsworth, M. D. S., Blehar, M. C., Waters, E. and Wall, S. (1978) *Patterns of Attachment: A psychological study of the strange situation*, Hillsdale, NJ: Erlbaum.

Bowlby, J. (1951) *Maternal Care and Mental Health*, Geneva: World Health Organization.

Bowlby, J. (1979) *The Making and Breaking of Affectional Bonds*, London: Tavistock Publications.

Bowlby, J. (1988) *A Secure Base: Clinical application of attachment theory*, London: Routledge.

George, C., Kaplan, N. and Main, M. (1985) *The Adult Attachment Interview*, Unpublished manuscript, Berkeley: University of California.

Grossmann, K. E. and Grossmann K. (1991) 'Attachment quality as an organizer of emotional and behavioural responses in a longitudinal perspective', in Parkes, C. M., Hinde, J. S. and Marris, P. *Attachment Across the Life Cycle* (pp 93-114), London: Routledge.

Macaskill, C. (1985) *Against the Odds: Adopting mentally handicapped children*, London: BAAF.

Main, M. (1990) 'Cross-cultural studies of attachment organization: recent studies, changing methodologies and the concept of conditional strategies', in *Human Development* 33, pp 48-61.

Main, M., Kaplan, N. and Cassidy, J. (1985) 'Security in infancy, childhood and adulthood: A move to the level of representation', in Bretherton, I. and Waters, E. (eds) *Growing points in attachment theory and research*, pp 66-104, Monographs of the Society for Research in Child Development 50, Serial No. 209.

Main, M. and Goldwyn, R. (in press) 'Adult attachment rating and classification systems', in Main, M. (ed) *A typology of human attachment organization assessed in discourse, drawings and interviews* (working title), New York: Cambridge University Press.

Sroufe, L. A. (1988) 'The role of infant-caregiver attachment in development', in Belsky, J. and Nezworski, T. (eds) *Clinical Implications of Attachment*, pp 18-38, Hillsdale, NJ: Erlbaum.

Living with siblings who have been sexually abused: Implications for assessment and support

MARIAN ELGAR
Guardian *ad litem*
Senior Lecturer
Oxford Brookes
University
ANN HEAD
Guardian *ad litem*

Title and aims of research

From Court Process to Care Plan: An empirical study of the placement of sexually abused children

Despite the research guidelines, reflected in the Children Act 1989, that sibling groups should be placed together, practice experience has suggested that there could be special difficulties in placing sexually abused siblings together. The aims of the study were to test out this hypothesis and to examine current practice in relation to placements after the end of care proceedings.

This paper is limited to the focus of 'living with siblings who have been sexually abused – implications for assessment and support'.

Method

An initial group of children who had been subject to care proceedings formed the sample group. Some of these children had returned home following court proceedings, others were placed in substitute care. All the children in the sample group had been seriously sexually abused within the family or were brothers or sisters of children who had been sexually abused and all were members of a sibling group.

The grounds for the actual care proceedings varied and included physical or emotional abuse or neglect; in some cases sexual abuse emerged as a serious issue only after the children were removed from home. Retrospective interviews were conducted with the carers of the children at different stages; short-term carers during and after the proceedings and, where the children had remained in care, their long term carers or adoptive parents. Some remained at home or returned to their original or differently constituted families. Some children were placed in residential establishments and key members of staff were interviewed in these cases.

Sample

The sample group included 85 children of whom 60 per cent were girls and 40 per cent boys between the ages of 1 to 16 years. The children came from a total of 37 sibling groups. Interviews were conducted with 86 carers of the children. The children themselves were not interviewed. This is a relatively small sample but nevertheless one that can be helpful in considering practice guidelines.

Major findings

Summary

- A large percentage of the children were separated from one or more siblings.

- The majority of the children were placed in permanent substitute homes.

- A strong association was found between children who had suffered serious sexual abuse and the propensity of those children to abuse other children.

- Many carers were unprepared for the consequences of sexual abuse.

- Carers who made a close bond with children were often able to withstand severe behavioural problems.

- Contact with birth families was typically much less than envisaged at the conclusion of care proceedings.

- Contact with birth parents was stressful for carers and usually infrequent. Contact with siblings was less problematic unless the siblings remained living in the family home.

- There was very little indirect contact which involved the children.

A large percentage of the children were separated from one or more siblings

In the study of 85 children (all of whom were part of a sibling group) 61 were separated from one or more of their siblings at the end of care proceedings. This was a high number of separations of children from their brothers and sisters; about three quarters of the children were separated from one or more siblings.

This was for a number or reasons:

- in some cases, some but not all members of the family were removed from home – separations in this case were made by legal intervention.

- for those children who were removed from home, some were separated on placement and it was unusual for those siblings to be reunited

- some of the separations were made deliberately in response to the children's needs

- in some cases "lack of resources" had caused the separation – this was usually the inability of foster carers to take a large sibling group.

Overall, the picture for the younger age group was one of family units being placed in couples of children and with an occasional single child placed alone. The older children were more likely to be separated and placed alone and, of this group, a number spent time in therapeutic establishments.

Implications for assessment of children
Reasons for separations
Practitioners need to be clear when siblings are separated what the rationale is or was behind this and whether it related to the harm the child had suffered or whether the decisions were taken pragmatically.

Different sorts of children: different sibling relationships
Some of the children in the study had been physically and emotionally abused and neglected. These children were typically described as having considerable special needs. Other children had been sexually abused within a caring relationship and there had not been incidents of physical abuse and neglect; these children often had great problems in coming to terms with the abuse and with their feelings of guilt and rejection.

Where a child was the only child of the family to be removed from home, as a result of a disclosure of sexual abuse, there were particular difficulties in relation to settling in an alternative placement and in maintaining contact with parents and siblings. If the child had been "scapegoated" by parents as a result of his or her disclosure, a not uncommon situation, it became very difficult to establish good quality contact with siblings in their parents' presence. The researchers felt that attention should be given, in these cases, to arranging contact for the siblings separately from the parents.

It became apparent that the information available initially when the child comes into care changes with time, sometimes little by little as the child becomes better known – the assessment process therefore can be a slow one. It seems important therefore to be able to understand the sibling relationships within as short a time frame as possible so that the impact of separation on the children can be taken into account in the assessment – that means having as clear an understanding of the dynamics of the family of origin as is possible.

The majority of the children were placed in permanent substitute homes
A high percentage of the children were made the subject of care orders by comparison with national statistics of court orders made, suggesting that child sexual abuse is treated more seriously than other reasons for placing children in public care.

At the conclusion of care proceedings the majority of the children were placed in foster care (46 of the 85 children). The care plan, at the conclusion of care proceedings, was for 37 of the children (43%), to be placed either in long-term foster care or in foster care with a view to adoption. By the time that interviews were conducted with carers (between two and four years later) the care plans remained as planned for 29 children (46%; N=54). For the remainder of the children the plans had been changed. More children were now expected to be placed for adoption and correspondingly less children were to be rehabilitated with their natural families.

Implications for assessment of children and families
The changes to care plans noted above highlighted the need for more thorough care plans, based on assessments before the final hearing.

Practitioners will be well aware that such changes have taken place in the years since these particular plans were made and there are much higher expectations of the local authority's care plan since the case decisions (*Re T* and *Re J*) made in 1994.

A strong association was found between children who had suffered serious sexual abuse and the propensity of those children to abuse other children

The children in our sample were all children who were thought to have been sexually abused within the family or they were brothers and sisters of children who had been sexually abused. In the questionnaire we included questions which gave a good indication of the seriousness of this abuse. There was a strong association between children who had been seriously abused and the propensity of those children to abuse other children.

The typical scenario was one in which quite young children, placed together with their siblings, were continuing to have sexual contact which, in many cases, appeared to have gone unnoticed by the carers. The reason this had gone unnoticed was firstly that some of the children came into the care system for reasons other than sexual abuse. It was only when they were settled that they disclosed sexual abuse – so in these cases an abusive relationship was not anticipated. Secondly, even where the history of sexual abuse was known, foster carers, especially of the younger children, were unprepared for the children to re-enact previous sexual experiences with their siblings. And thirdly, it was common for carers to be unaware of the history of abuse to the children in their care and once again, therefore, sexual behaviour was not anticipated.

Implications for assessment of children

To be able to care for and protect the children it is important for carers to have an accurate account of the child's experience of sexual abuse if this is available and to understand the propensity of such children to abuse. Carers need to be aware of the context for the child, the degree of violence involved, and whether children from the same family had been treated similarly or differently. This information is an important part of the assessment of the child and it helps in understanding their reactions and coping mechanisms.

It goes without saying that young children living in a family home who are likely to abuse other children present problems of management for the carers as the children cannot be left alone with their siblings and in many cases they present a danger to others in the household – the carer's children, visiting children, or in some cases children at school.

It follows from this that carers must be given full information about the background of the children in their care, including information about previous sexual abuse. Many carers did not appear to have this information, for reasons which were not made clear, but may have included concerns about confidentiality.

It is proposed that assessment and training of foster carers should include an emphasis on the need for strict confidentiality in relation to these sensitive but crucial matters, thereby increasing the confidence of local authorities to share such information.

Many carers were unprepared for the consequences of sexual abuse

The difficulties of caring for the children, as described above, led some carers, when asked, to wonder whether the children in their care would have been better placed as an only child in the family or with siblings. A surprising 31 per cent thought that individual children would have been better placed on their own in foster care. This seemed to be either because they felt that the children had such overwhelming needs that they required one-to-one relationships or because a strong bond had been made by the carers with one child but not with a sibling or siblings. There are some complex issues concerned here. In terms of separation of siblings there is considerable evidence that brothers and sisters fulfil important roles for each other in terms of identity, learning about social relationships, and often in providing support and companionship in later life (Banks and Kahn, 1982; Dunn, 1993). These are all strong reasons for placing siblings together. Some of the carers, however, thought that placement with siblings perpetuated the dysfunctional relationships in the family of origin – this being particularly true where there was sexual activity between the children. The carers sometimes felt that each individual child had such huge problems the carers could not meet the emotional needs of more than one child. This applied also in terms of the multiplicity of appointments with professionals to which the children needed to be accompanied.

There is also a third point: in considering the needs of each child individually it can happen that the needs of one child to be placed alone may be in conflict with the needs of their sibling for whom joint placement is considered the preferred option.

Implications for assessment and support of carers

The enormity of the task faced by carers of sibling groups who have experienced sexual abuse is appreciated and there may be some siblings who cannot be successfully cared for together. In making this decision, however, the authors think that there are advantages, in the long term for the children, if the dysfunctional sibling relationships can be addressed within the placement. This presupposes that the carers have some understanding of the natural family dynamics. It was noticeable that of the carers who thought separate placements would have been right for the children, almost all said this would only have been possible early on; once the children were settled in their placement they thought it no longer feasible.

Carers who made a close bond with children were often able to withstand severe behavioural problems

The carers included both short and long-term carers and some adoptive families. Not surprisingly many of the short-term carers were very experienced and had fostered a large number of individual children. Although some of these placements did not last as long as required, most of the short-term carers were able to manage the very difficult behaviour that the children presented initially, which included a spectrum of behaviour: tantrums, sulking, dissociated behaviour, soiling and smearing, poor concentration; there was a high proportion of children with learning difficulties and children with statements of educational need.

Some of the short-term carers established attachments with the children and some extraordinarily difficult children remained in their first placements; a key issue for the carers was the bond they had made with the child. The assumption was that there was a reciprocation of trust between carers and the child where the carer had been an adult to whom the child was able to talk about their experiences of abuse; this assumption was based on the experiences of some carers. The vulnerability in the child seems to have allowed for the beginnings of deep attachments to develop and, where this happened, in some cases the children were able to stay on with their "short-term" carers. Recent work in America by Katz (1996), currently being piloted by the Manchester Adoption Society, and in the UK by Clatworthy (1997) and others on "concurrent planning" is building on the hypothesis that it is damaging to break these relationships if the child is unable to return home.

However, there were children in this situation who had made reciprocated attachments but who were nevertheless moved on. One child who had become well attached to her foster mother was moved to a long-term family and whereas her younger sister settled well, the older child did not appear to be able to reproduce the affection and trust of her original placement.

Planning for sibling groups caused delay in some cases. In the worst case one family waited for four years from the outset of care proceedings for placement – there were multiple reasons for this but amongst them was the need to plan for a large sibling group and the children's very difficult behaviour. In this family the sexualised element of the children's behaviour was not appreciated until they were in a permanent placement.

However, some of the permanent placements were with what might be considered to be traditional adoptive families – families who were childless and wishing to create their own family unit through adoption. These families had little previous experience of caring for children and there is no doubt some encountered major problems – it was often the determination, dedication and perseverance of these adoptive families which held the placements together rather than their experience or the support they were offered from without.

Implications for assessment of children
Assessments of the sibling relationships and of attachment needs of the children were vital in determining the right placements. A difficult balance was required between the needs of individual children for close relationships with one or more adults and their needs for their siblings. Key in this was an assessment of attachments to current carers, and an understanding of the sibling relationships. This underlines the difficulties in assessments – on the one hand the need to understand the children and their history, which takes time, and on the other hand to lose no time in making important decisions.

Contact with birth families was typically much less than envisaged at the conclusion of care proceedings
Contact in permanent placements was usually between once and four times a year. Contact with siblings was more likely to be well maintained when the children were all in care albeit in different placements. Where siblings remained at home with their birth families it was unusual for there to be separate sibling contact and this was included in the contact with birth parents if there was any.

Contact with birth parents was stressful for carers and usually infrequent. Contact with siblings was less problematic unless the siblings remained living in the family home

Carers seemed to find contact stressful because they thought it was emotionally damaging for the children; this was because in some cases the children seemed to regress after contact. There was no ongoing contact in any adoptive placements apart from one. In this case the contact was considered to be beneficial all round. For the individual sibling who had been removed from home and placed in foster care, contact was particularly difficult.

Many long-term foster carers and adoptive parents continued with indirect contact with the birth parents. There were few instances where this was reciprocated and, although the indirect contact may have benefited the birth parents, the children received no benefit, in the sense of having up-to-date information about their original family.

Implications for assessment and support of carers

Contact for children in care with their siblings who remain in the family home seemed to be given little attention. It was seldom separated from contact with parents and it may be worthwhile to consider maintaining this contact separately from birth parent contact as it seems to have advantages. Firstly, contact with siblings was seen by the carers as generally less problematic than contact with parents and secondly, sibling contact is (it is assumed) as effective in maintaining identity links as contact with parents.

Such contact with siblings as there was, was seldom planned for the benefit of the sibling relationship. Enjoyable and meaningful school holiday contact between siblings could be effective and workable and it could help to understand the changing family patterns. Supervision of the contact should be borne in mind.

It is accepted that contact with birth parents is important but it was found in our sample that the contact was problematic for the reasons already outlined. Contact for these very damaged children has an emotional content for the children and also for the carers. There was a view from carers that it was not acceptable for the children to be upset by contact, and this was used as an argument against contact. However, no carers said that they, rather than the children, were upset by the prospect of contact and that this might have an influence on the child. It might be helpful for carers to be allowed to acknowledge their own feelings about the contact and the impact this has on the child.

Another point about which there was little direct information was the help that was offered to parents in preparation for contact. Inappropriate behaviour by the parents at contact was an issue, as was an apparent lack of interest in the child. Possibly an important aspect for contact was the degree of help that was given to parents in preparation for it – information which they might have when "partnership" is working well, social work support in understanding the child's needs and developmental stage, and help in ways of expressing the changes in their own family in a way appropriate to their child. It was especially difficult for parents or relatives to maintain contact where it was reduced to a few hours a year and families were inevitably out of touch with the child. Ongoing support would greatly assist in the quality of contact.

When the time scales in the reduction of contact between children and their parents were considered it seemed that the planned contact was quickly reduced to a "manageable" level. Whether this was necessary or desirable in all cases is uncertain particularly as experience of private law situations, such as cited by Maclean and Ekelaar (1997), suggests that contact can improve if it is persevered with and, with time, the animosity can reduce and a reasonable relationship can be arrived at between the parents. So possibly, in public law cases, if the parents are given time to adjust to the loss of the child they may be able to make a positive contribution for the child at a later stage. This may well have relevance to public law situations. Cutting contact to a minimum at an early stage does not allow that possibility.

There was very little indirect contact which involved the children
Finally if indirect contact is to be for the benefit to the child, the birth family needs to be given help and support to be able to continue with this; the support should be part of a post adoption package. Without this it is only resourceful and determined parents who are able to continue.

Conclusions

There are a number of interesting links between this research and other recent work, some of which confirms or supports the findings. In terms of practice developments, the theoretical underpinning of "concurrent planning" is based on the premise that even where plans are uncertain for the child, helping children to attach can be a way towards permanence, whether or not the child is able to return home. These ideas have arisen out of a recognition of the detrimental effects on children of encouraging and then breaking their attachments to carers. Equally, Rushton and Mayes (1997) have been interested in how to promote attachment in children placed in substitute care.

The suggestion that an understanding of the dynamics of the child's birth family is essential for the placement to be effective is complimentary to the systemic family approach to foster care assessment recently proposed by McCracken and Reilley (1998).

References

Clatworthy, B. (1997) 'Concurrent Planning', *Seen and Heard*, Vol 7 Dec.

Banks, S. P. and Kahn, M. D. (1982) *The Sibling Bond*, New York: Basic Books.

Dunn, J. (1993) *Young Children's Close Relationships beyond Attachment*, Newbury Park California: Sage.

Katz, L. (1996) 'Permanency Action through Concurrent Planning', in *Adoption & Fostering*, 20 : 2.

McCracken, S. and Reilley, I. (1998) 'The systemic family approach to foster care assessment', in *Adoption & Fostering*, 22 : 3.

Maclean, M. and Ekelaar, J. (1997) *The Parental Obligation: A study of cross household parenting*, Oxford: Hart.

Rushton, A. and Mayes, D. (1997) 'Forming Fresh Attachments in Childhood: A research update', in *Child and Family Social Work*, 2 : 2, pp 121-127, May.

Re T (a minor) (care order; conditions) [(1994)] FLR 423

Re J (minors) (care plan) [(1994)] FLR 253

Developing a research methodology for social work assessment in adoption and fostering

DEREK CLIFFORD

Senior Lecturer in
Social Work
Liverpool John Moores
University

Abstract

The paper is based on research into the theory and practice of assessment over several years in the North West. Involvement in research with practitioners has highlighted the parallel processes of assessment and research. Related studies in research methodology and social theory enabled the development of a "critical auto/biographical" theoretical framework which provides a basis for research and social assessment which, in fostering and adoption, can encompass the processes of assessment, preparation and support into placement. The framework both supports and extends practice wisdom but also provides a basis for critique and development of assessment practices.

Introduction

The occasion for inviting me to this research conference has been the publication last year of two papers about assessment and research processes in fostering and adoption (Clifford and Cropper, 1997a and 1997b). However, these papers were originally written over two years prior to that date, and based on research done even earlier in 1992–3. More significantly, several other related papers have been published in relation to this research (Clifford, 1994; 1995; Clifford and Cropper, 1994; Cropper, 1997) – including work which was never intended to be limited to the fields of adoption and fostering (nor to that of empirical research). The culmination of this effort of reading and researching over several years has been the recent publication of a book (Clifford, 1998a) and some associated CD Rom software (Clifford, 1998b) about social assessment theory and practice. This conference paper – and the paper which has occasioned it – should thus both be understood as part of a wider strategy which underpins the justification and intention of this paper, although its focus is on the work done in fostering and adoption.

Research methodology and social theory as pre-requisites of good practice

Practitioners understandably do not always want to know about the detailed methodology of a piece of research because they are primarily interested in the research results and their implications for practice. However, in this research it is the methods used by workers to make assessments of social situations and the justification of those methods that were being discussed, whilst simultaneously the researchers had to justifiy their own methods to research the social interactions involved in doing assessments. Both practitioners and researchers are thus being asked to reflect explicitly upon their own assumptions – the conceptual framework that they use in day-to-day practice, and the extent to which it could be justified and how far it needed clarification and development. In addition, the users, or in this case the potential carers, experiencing the assessment process were asked to reflect upon the methods used and how they perceived their meaning and adequacy.

In the earlier research we concentrated on the process of assessing potential foster and adoptive *carers* partly because that was a relatively accessible set of procedures, but also because it raised particular concerns and issues, for example, the question of the extent to which the assessing social worker could claim "expertise" at all in relation to judgements about the future caring potential of the applicants, and how this could be justifed or managed. It also had the great advantage that it was possible to interview directly the "consumers" of the assessment processes as well as the "producers" of assessments. We used focus group and life history interviewing of workers and carers in two organisations – one a voluntary adoption agency and the other the fostering and adoption specialists of a social services department. We were thus able to look at diverse processes and agencies from a variety of angles with differing degrees of participant involvement at different stages, trying to understand the methods and values that underpinned assessment.

The message in recent years from commentators both inside and outside social work is that the theoretical framework underpinning assessment is either absent or inadequate. The psychiatrist Peter Reder has made significant contributions to the assessment of children and families in recent years, and the 1995 collection on the *assessment of parenting* is particularly relevant in fostering and adoption for both carers and natural parents. In the introductory chapter it is stressed that a theoretical framework is essential to assessment. They comment bluntly that the problem with social work assessment based on the "Orange Book" (Department of Health, 1988), is that the latter: ' ... contains an extensive list of recommended questions but provides no theoretical framework to help ' ... make sense of the answers' (Reder and Lucey, 1995, p.5). A recent paper on social work assessment agrees that the problem is that: ' ... there is no conceptual framework which adequately embraces the range of assessment tasks' (Lloyd and Taylor, 1995). The latest summary of the use of theory in adoption indicates a traditional eclecticism (Triseliotis, 1997, p.141), but recent DoH research confirms the unacceptable deficiency of theory in social work assessments (Farmer and Owen, 1995, Ch 9).

The theoretical framework that was used for this research had been developed over a period of time from 1988, beginning with the publication of two earlier papers (Clifford, 1992/3 and 1994). The latter paper presented the concept of "critical life histories" as a key anti-oppressive research method for use by professionals in social welfare and health. The intention was that social work assessment in particular would benefit from such a conceptual basis because it is based on methods akin to oral history and life history methods in sociology and history. This orientation towards the perspectives of various oppressed groups in relation to social theory and research methodology has continued to be explored and has been reframed as a "critical auto/biographical" framework for assessment (Clifford, 1998a). This emphasises the element of reflexive participation by the assessor or researcher in understanding critically the issues of power and oppression in someone else's life history and its impact on the present and future. This development was influenced by the significant contribution of lesbian feminists and others to social theory and research methodology (eg. Stanley, 1992; Stanley and Wise, 1983 and 1994).

Following the research into fostering and adoption, a new team of colleagues began to work on applying the concepts to child protection work, in association with a social services department. We developed a method of co-researching with workers in the department which gave them access to our ideas, and gave us access to their experience – by means of combining training and research. We have offered training in the use of these concepts of assessment, and related them to a range of available pro formas and schedules for assessment. Workers completed questionnaires and discussed in focus groups the relevance and usefulness of the concepts to the tasks they were attempting to complete in relation to child protection. It is planned that the theoretical framework that has been developed will be explored again in connection with fostering and adoption, but this time a proposal has been developed to include the study of the comprehensive and long-term planning assessments done by field social workers. This will be supported by adoption agencies interested to know how decisions are made to use or not to use their services.

As argued in the previous papers, and elaborated more fully in the recent book, the basic principles of a theoretical framework suitable for social work assessment are drawn from perspectives of oppressed groups which are interpreted in the light of current social theory and research methodology. Working in partnership or empowering users and carers must include taking seriously the need to integrate their perspectives into the methodology of assessment. Thus each of the basic principles has to be taken together and inter-related as part of a value-based methodology. This research was instrumental in engendering a useful transition towards a broad theoretical framework for social assessment which is now summarised in the current book (Clifford, 1998a). It is argued that a theoretical framework for a *social* assessment (as against a medical or psychological assessment) is a requirement of all social work assessments: the basic concepts or principles apply equally to work with children or with older people (Clifford, 1995; 1996). However, in this paper I will review the specific principles of this framework mainly in the light of a recent authoritative introduction to the theory, policy and practice of adoption (Triseliotis, *et al*, 1997). Published at the same time as the papers reporting this research, it reflects good practice based on approximately the same period of historical time.

Practitioner and user perspectives on assessment theory

The reference to Triseliotis (*et al*) is relevant because whilst its account of assessment practices does broadly correspond to the picture discovered in our research, it does not evaluate the practices described in the light of a theoretical framework. It recommends the use of an eclectic mixture of theoretical concepts and practices that corresponds well to what was actually being used. What I aim to do here is to use the framework (partially) developed in researching adoption and fostering assessment to question and develop further the practice described in a book which is an influential point of reference. I will thus pick up on the evidence previously presented about the theoretical framework (in the papers cited) but discuss it in the context of continuing representations of how assessment in this kind of setting should be done. The point is that both in the original research and in the recent authoritative literature on assessment processes in adoption similar strengths and weaknesses are manifest. Taking each of the basic concepts of a critical auto/biographical theoretical framework for assessment in turn, the paper will demonstrate how practical issues can be usefully scrutinised within this context.

Power

The concept of power is fundamental to any adequate social theory, and recent discussions by feminists and others have emphasised the pervasive nature of power generated in discourses of knowledge, in which professional assessments are directly implicated, and the multi-dimensional aspects of power (Clifford, 1998a, Chapter 6). In making assessments a rigorous and well-informed concept of power is needed to analyse the various aspects of human social behaviour and the development of needs and risks. There are institutional, organisational, local and central, personal, economic and political aspects to power which impinge on assessment in a bewildering variety of ways. The positive and negative implications of power relationships are key issues for the welfare of children and this should be central to assessment considerations. Farmer and Owen (1995) stress the importance of reflecting on changing power relationships in assessment, especially after child protection conferences when carers' reliance on social workers' opinions can dramatically alter, with serious consequences for children in their care (p.260). In adoption and fostering assessments, potential carers' power *also* gradually increases through the process. In both cases one of the ethical and political requirements is to work in partnership with carers, and this is especially the case for potential carers who are offering a valuable service to children and to agencies. However, there is a balance to be maintained between workers using their power legitimately to establish the possibilities of risk, the range of need or the potential for caring, as against interventions in people's lives which are unjustifiably intrusive and fail to recognise, support and develop their strengths.

Triseliotis *et al* present assessment of carers as a matter of preparation and matching with relatively little emphasis on the responsibility to use power to investigate and assess potential carers to ensure the welfare of children. The recent publication of fresh guidelines on "dangerous caring" emphasises once again that there are a number of factors which may indicate the presence of risks, many by means of a detailed historical study of personal and family lives (Dent, 1998). Nor is there any emphasis in the evidence from our research, nor in the summary of good practice by Triseliotis *et al*, that the "home study" needs to *verify or disconfirm* the picture of family and personal history that applicants have given: the model of working together tends to assume that the interests of both parties are the same. This ignores the growing power of applicants to "read" social workers' expectations and give the required answers: a possibility that carers mentioned themselves and was previously reported in the research. However, carers themselves have indicated in our research that there have been serious matters, such as mental health treatment, deliberately hidden from social workers (Clifford and Cropper, 1997b p.241). More comprehensively, the power issues that generate needs, risks and strengths should be examined in detail for all relevant individuals, whose current balance of needs and strengths may be altered dramatically by the placement of a child with a different range of needs, abilities and vulnerabilities to the relative powers of carers and families.

The discussion of group *work* in Triseliotis *et al* (op cit., p.144) corresponds with our research finding that social workers were not clear about the assessment content of such sessions, and great stress was being placed on education and experiential sharing of ideas by potential carers. However, the research indicated that applicants were aware of informal assessment by workers during group sessions, and felt they had to conform to expected norms in these circumstances (Clifford and Cropper, 1997b p.242). The point is that the structure of the power situation in these group sessions is such that the applicants correctly surmise that they will be assessed, whatever is formally said. Ironically, the concept of empowerment may itself be used to obscure the realities and responsibilities of power (cf Humphries, 1996). Social workers need to recognise the reality of their own position in the power structure and legitimise its use through open recognition of the inevitable fact of assessment, and through being clear about the criteria. The situation is parallel to that in child protection where there is the highly complex issue of: 'balancing state intervention and family autonomy' (Seden, Hardiker and Barker, 1996), but with the added major complication of expecting and encouraging the increasing empowerment of carers towards family and group self-sufficiency, and the status of service providers and colleagues. These issues cannot be resolved in simplistic ways, but require the professional judgement of workers to be exercised within a theoretical framework, part of which requires an understanding of the multiple and interactive dimensions of power.

Historical location

The concept of seeing potential carers in terms of personal, family and social history is a traditional method that workers have rightly used for a long time to enable both parties to understand better their caring capacities; what kind of backgrounds they have, and when and where their attitudes towards children and other relevant issues have been formed. What they have also tended to do (along with all other social workers) is to rely on psychological and psychodynamic theories to justify the social history. My contention is that there are more important theoretical resources for constructing social histories, such as sociological life histories and oral history, as well as life span psychologies which are beginning to acknowledge more fully the importance of the social and historical dimensions of psychology (eg Burman, 1997). This argument is spelt out in detail elsewhere (Clifford, 1998a, Ch 4), but the main point here is that that although psychological theories of attachment are an important basis for assessment in adoption and fostering, the interpretation of relationship dynamics needs to be placed within a social and historical framework independently of a psychological theory of development.

Triseliotis *et al* again mirror the findings of our research in that concepts of attachment and psychodynamic theory were indeed often reflected in workers' comments about their assumptions in assessment, particularly in their study of carers as children. However, some potential carers reflected upon the ways in which the history-taking of workers was unevenly skewed towards their childhood. They acknowledged the interest of workers not just in their psychological development but in the origins of their concepts of childhood and parenting. However, they also felt that a lot of important information about them was not picked up because their histories in more recent times were passed over rapidly. The whole range of personal and family history needs to be examined in relation to the changing strengths and needs of potential carers and their families, to identify risk factors in specific histories, and equally to be accurate about strengths, and how they have been influenced directly and indirectly by wider aspects of social history. Understanding reactions to these changing circumstances will be the key to evaluating the continuing changes through child placement and the development of a new family. In other words, the auto/biography of people's lives is an *historical* study which requires equal attention to a whole series of social transitions. This social history provides the context for any narrower developmental psychological or psychiatric assessment which might need to be made: individuals and families are thus assessed within a concrete historical location.

Further issues about the place of historical location in assessment concern the linkages between past, present and future in the processes of assessment themselves. It is clear that the process of assessment through to placement and beyond always takes place over a considerable period of time, and that there will be changes in perception on both sides, and changes in potential related to the assessment process itself. However, the process is presented as a 'task-centred' event (Triseliotis *et al*, *op cit*, p.141), with completion of the tasks (especially BAAF Form F and group training) as events which are relatively autonomous and not necessarily seen in a dynamic historical context either in relation to each other or to past or future states. However, these processes themselves are part of the social histories through which individual and group behaviours change and develop into the period of placement. Continual re-assessment and historical location would seem to be more relevant concepts. For example, how have people reacted to the group preparation process and the home study – and what is the significance of their relationship in time? How far do carers develop their understanding over time – or simply repeat what is expected? How do their reactions to placement compare with their performance during assessment? What continuities and discontinuities can be perceived between any of these stages? There are similar criticisims to be made of the "Orange Book" (DoH, 1988), which also takes a relatively static snapshot view of people's lives (Clifford, 1998a, p.144). Again, the professional judgement of the worker is required to make a social assessment using an informed theoretical framework in which historical location is a key concept.

Interacting social systems

Systems theory has been widely appreciated in assessment work in adoption and fostering particularly in its application to family systems (McCracken and Reilly, 1998). Triseliotis *et al* rightly point to the importance of systems concepts in analysing not only family and extended family but also neighbourhood and other environmental variables for evidence of either supportive or stressful factors, particularly through the use of ecomaps and other techniques (Triseliotis *et al*, 1998, p.153). Nevertheless, its theory has sometimes been found wanting in relation to the inclusion of key concepts such as power, historical change, and social difference, and it is still a widely debated issue in contemporary social theory (Clifford, 1998a, Ch. 5).

In adoption and fostering there are numerous social sytems which are in constant flux through time. Whilst the genogram may display the origins of family systems, and the ecomap indicate current tensions and supports, it is an important part of social assessment to grasp the way various systems change through the years, and through the process of assessment itself. In our research, applicants who had experienced the assessment process highlighted how much their family systems had changed in recent years, through various transitions, from being single to being a couple, and establishing their own homes and new networks independently of families of origin, and also how the assessment process itself had affected their social relationships and values (Clifford and Cropper, 1997a). The assessment of the interaction of social systems through time thus needs to go beyond the traditional ecomap and genogram approach. The use of preparation groups, and the assessment of this group as a system of interacting individuals, should impact on any assessment of individual performance within the groups, whilst the agency itself also develops and changes through time. The organisation has its own systemic issues of communication and control, developing policy, exercising authority and decision-making, and is involved in differing systemic relations of power. Our life history interviews with social workers illuminated their awareness of changing agency policies and structures and their roles within them, whilst applicants were able to tell stories about their experience of differing agency systems, as well as their processing through the current organisation and its perceived strengths and weaknesses.

The cultural and economic systems in which these agencies operate have a major influence on the expectations of assessing social workers and applicants. The wider social systems thus interact concurrently with the influence of smaller social systems and power issues pertaining to both require simultaneous consideration. The issues of influence and causation cannot be parcelled off to a psychological account of individual development, a systemic account of family relationships, and an ecomap of "environmental" social systems. The influence of wider social systems has to be taken into account in assessing the individual person as a social being as well as the social systems of the family, the agency, and the group. This is another aspect of the way the social contextualises the psychological – through social as well as historical space. It has been suggested that the over-use of attachment theory in adoption and fostering arises because of this focus on the psychology of the nuclear family, and the overlooking of the existence and maintenance of multiple social links of less intensity – especially in relation to oppressed groups and their extended family and community systems (O'Shaughnessy, 1994). In both cases, whether social system supports or stresses are being considered the analysis of the various systems has to be combined together in specific historical contexts, and with the implications of power – ability and vulnerability built into the analysis. The professional judgement of workers thus draws on concepts of system which are not only informed by recent debates in social theory but are linked to the other key concepts as part of a theoretical framework for social assessment compatible with the perspectives of oppressed and user groups.

Social difference
Although social differences in respect of the major social divisions have long been taken seriously in social assessments, their application has been fragmentary and incomplete, sometimes emphasising one social category

then another. More recently, the nature of the various categories and their inter-relationship have been criticised from a postmodernist perspective. However, this is all the more reason for attempting to give systematic consideration to the complexity of social division in relation to specific social situations (Clifford, 1998a, Ch. 2). In social work assessment pro-formas, the various social divisions make spasmodic appearances, and in Triseliotis' work there are similarly occasional references to one or another social division. However, the critical auto/biographical framework developed problematises the concepts and suggests a thorough consideration of all the possibilities within social situations, contextualising difference within historical and political dimensions.

In fostering and adoption assessments, social difference surrounds all participants in the process. In particular, the fundamental difference of age between the adults being assessed and the child being placed underpins the proper concern of social workers and agencies with the motives, attitudes and behaviour of potential carers towards children. The whole range of social divisions is relevant to the assessment of the applicants, not only for understanding who exactly they are, but their attitudes towards the natural parents are obviously of great importance to the child being placed, especially with the development of more open attitudes towards adoption, and the evidence of the value of contact in many cases in *fostering and adoption*. An understanding of the social identity of the applicants and their values and attitudes can be gained in a variety of ways – from evidence in groups, from personal interaction, but especially from the historical evidence of people's experience and reactions to events and trends in their lives and social circumstances. It has been previously noted that how individuals process and internalise values will depend on what has happened in their personal and family histories and their reactions to social events on wider structural as well as more intimate levels (Clifford and Cropper, 1997a). The most important point here is that the social divisions issues are not to be read as a kind of background environmental variable which occasionally encroach on the assessment. These social divisions are fundamentally constitutive of the immediate social relationships involved in the assessment including the interactions between workers and applicants in interview and group processes.

In our research there was plenty of evidence that people had varying degrees of awareness of social difference and its relevance to assessment, but neither applicants nor workers always reviewed the whole range of social divisions, or considered the full complexity of their implications for the assessment process. Some applicants were strongly aware of their status as educated middle class professionals who were critical of the whole process of being assessed either in groups or individually, and especially the difficulty of contributing to group sessions in a way that was sensitive to the very wide range of knowledge available. Other applicants were strongly aware of their status as gay, working class, black and/or disabled, especially when experienced in ways that their assessing social workers were not. They variously expressed reservations or made pointed comments about their consciousness of these social divisions and the implications for recruitment and assessment as potential carers. A positive feature was the appreciation by applicants of the individual and family assessment offered by experienced women workers: an outcome not unexpected from the perspective of this theoretical framework, since women have contributed significantly to the theory and practice of assessment. However, there were numerous discussions with both applicants and workers about social divisions where a variety of views were expressed with relatively little awareness of clear comprehensive guidelines. These conclusions were reinforced for the researchers in relation to their own membership of different social divisions and how this affected their research relationships. The need for professional judgement to be guided by a theoretical framework sensitive to the range of social division applied both to research and assessment.

Reflexivity

This concept is drawn from research methodologies where the observer is also seen as a participant whose personal values and perspectives are part of the interactional dynamics of the research process (Clifford, 1998a, Ch 3). This is highly relevant to any concept of social assessment, including that done in the areas of fostering and adoption. Social workers' membership of differing social positions, especially in relation to specific carers and users have to be evaluated. Their (changing) relative power and their personal experience of issues pertinent to the carers and users need to be taken into account in assessment processes. In adoption particularly, not only is the social worker's membership of all the social divisions an important issue which may affect the assessment process in various ways, but also the experience of infertility, or lack of it, resonates deeply with many applicants.

This concept is notable by its absence in Triseliotis *et al*, and this is reflected in some of the research evidence on which this paper is based. However, issues relating to reflexivity are reflected *indirectly* in Triseliotis *et al* in the contrast between the "inquisitorial approach" of social workers using the traditional psychodynamic investigative method (Triseliotis, *et al*, 1998, p.140), as compared to the current educative and partnership approaches in which the issues of reflexivity seem to disappear, since the social worker no longer appears to need to be making such explicit evaluative judgements. The ambiguity of this approach to the involvement of workers in assessment is evidenced in the views of workers that, despite the official policy that the use of Form F and the training sessions represented a relatively fair and "objective" assessment, in the end assessment was largely a matter of 'gut feeling and common sense', and more about the worker than about the applicant (Clifford and Cropper, 1997b, p. 241). On the other hand, applicants were often vocal in their views about the importance of the personal experience of social workers. Issues such as the following were raised with concern: whether the worker was a similar age and gender to the woman applicant; whether the worker shared similar social and/or religious values as the applicant; whether workers had personal experience of infertility; the gender of basic grade workers as against applicants generally, for example, the worker (on one occasion) being a young female in group discussions of infertility with men (Clifford and Cropper, 1997b, p.242). Thus whilst workers were unsure how to cope with this issue, applicants were very sure that it was important – though they were (unsurprisingly) selective about which kinds of personal experience were relevant to themselves. For example, "race" and ethnicity were sometimes conspicuous by their absence, and taken for granted by white applicants. Sexuality could be equally invisible – apart from the occasion when two male applicants were being assessed by a heterosexual worker. The implication of this theoretical framework is that such reflexive issues need to be made explicit and problematised by systematically considering the positions that workers hold within powerful organisations as well as their membership of all the social divisions and their differing experiences, and this is as relevant to group situations as to home studies. Such issues do not only apply of course to the basic grade workers doing the assessment, but the issues are equally relevant to management and other personnel who have crucial roles to play in the assessment process.

Conclusion

The above practical issues are only *some* of the issues that arose in the reported research and were mirrored directly or indirectly in the Triseliotis text. Since then, the reframing of the theory as a critical auto/biographical framework for social assessment provides a basis for re-examination of methods and assumptions (Clifford, 1998a). More recently the use of the framework to problematise and evaluate assessment pro formas such as risk assessment schedules and LAC documents has continued with the active involvement of social services personnel, and a basic CD Rom version of it has also been developed for use in training. It is not assumed that the development of this framework will provide neat answers, but so far it has met with the kind of response from workers that could be anticipated: it recognises the importance of what *social* workers are already doing in making *social* assessments, and provides a formal intellectual basis of support and a useful checklist of key concepts which helps them think through difficult issues of professional judgement.

References

Burman, E. (1997) 'Developmental psychology and its discontents', in Fox, D. and Prillentensky, I. (eds), *Critical Psychology: An introduction*, London: Sage.

Clifford, D. J. (1994) 'Critical life histories: a key anti-oppressive research method', in Humphries, B. and Trueman, C. (eds) *Rethinking Social Research*, London: Avebury.

Clifford, D. J. (1995) 'Methods in oral history and social work', *Oral History*, 24 : 2.

Clifford, D. J. (1996) 'Biography and social assessment in health and social services'. Paper presented to The Centre for Ageing and Biographical Studies at the Open University and The Centre for Policy on Ageing, London, June 21st.

Clifford, D. J. (1998a) *Social Assessment Theory and Practice: A multi-disciplinary framework*, Aldershot: Ashgate.

Clifford, D. J. (1998b) *Social Assessment Theory and Practice* (CD ROM Software), Liverpool: John Moores University.

Clifford, D. J. and Cropper, A. (1994) 'Applying auto/biography: researching the assessment of life experiences', in *Auto/Biography*, 3.1 and 3.2 (Double Issue), pp 47-58.

Clifford, D. J. and Cropper, A. (1997a) 'Individual assessment of potential carers: essential methods', in *Practice*, 9: 1.

Clifford, D. J. and Cropper, A. (1997b) 'Parallel processes in researching and assessing potential carers', in *Child and Family Social Work*, 2: 4.

Cropper, A. (1995) *Applying a Black Feminist Approach to Social Work Assessment*, Unpublished M.Phil Dissertation, Liverpool: John Moores University.

Cropper, A. (1997) 'Rethinking Practice: Learning from a Black Feminist Perspective', in Bates, J., Pugh, R. and Thompson N. (eds) *Protecting Children: Challenges and Changes*, Arena.

Dent, R. J. (1998) *Dangerous Care: Working to protect children*, The Bridge Child Care Development Service, London.

Department of Health (1988) *Protecting Children: A guide for social workers undertaking a comprehensive assessment*, HMSO: London.

Farmer, E. and Owen, M. (1995) *Child Protection Practice: Private risks and public remedies*, HMSO: London.

Humphries, B. (1996) 'Contradictions in the culture of empowerment', in Humphries B (ed), *Critical Perspectives on Empowerment*, Birmingham: Venture Press.

Lloyd, M. and Taylor C. (1995) 'From Hollis to the Orange Book: Developing a holistic model of social work assessment in the 1990s', in *British Journal of Social Work*, 25 : 6.

McCracken, S. and Reilly, R. (1998) 'The systemic family approach to foster care assessment: A review and update', in *Adoption & Fostering*, 22 : 3.

O'Shaughnessy, T. (1994) *Adoption, Social Work and Social Theory*, Aldershot : Avebury, (1998).

Reder, P. and Lucey C. (eds) (1995) *Assessment of Parenting: Psychiatric and psychological contributions*, London: Routledge.

Stanley, L. and Wise, S. (1983) *Breaking Out*, Manchester : Manchester University Press.

Stanley L. (1992) *The Auto/Biographical I*, Manchester : Manchester University Press.

Stanley, L. and Wise, S. (1994) *Breaking Out Again*, Manchester : Manchester University Press.

Triseliotis, J., Shireman, J. and Hundleby, M. (1997) *Adoption: Theory, policy and practice*, London: Cassell.

Sibling research and practice implications for placement decisions

AUDREY MULLENDER
Professor of Social Work
University of Warwick

ANITA PAVLOVIC
Lecturer in Sociology
Nene College
Northampton

Introduction

The first part of this chapter will offer a brief outline of the findings from a study of birth siblings on the Adoption Contact Register for England and Wales. It will then go on to explore common themes emerging from a range of papers on siblings being submitted by researchers, practitioners and those personally involved to an edited collection (Mullender, 1999, forthcoming). The idea for this book arose at the BAAF Research Symposium in 1997 – when it became clear that there was a gap in the literature and that there was a great need for such material to be offered to practitioners and policy makers. The content covers not just adoption but also siblings in all parts of the care system.

The birth sibling study

The research on birth siblings on the Adoption Contact Register arose from an earlier study of all birth relatives using Part II of the Register (Mullender and Kearn, 1997), from which it emerged that the second largest group (Table 1), after birth mothers, was siblings. Out of 1,784 respondents to the original study, 347 (or almost 1 in 5) were siblings. They also represented the widest spread of ages, with smaller groups in their 20s and over 60, and the rest fairly evenly distributed in their 30s, 40s, and 50s. Consequently, the experiences of these birth siblings related to all the eras of adoption, from the early days, then through the war years, and on into the peak of placements during the "sexual revolution" of the 1960s and beyond.

This discovery of so many siblings, and with such a range of backgrounds, was an interesting finding in itself – all the more so because there was no literature on adult siblings separated by adoption to compare with that on relinquishing birth mothers and they had been a largely invisible group up to this time. It became apparent that an in-depth study, purely of siblings' perceptions and experiences, would be a rich new vein to mine. In particular, we, as the researchers, were fascinated to learn why people were keen to trace their adult adopted siblings, sometimes without ever having met them before (where, for example, a child had been born out of wedlock and placed some years before the subsequent child was even born).

Clearly, for reasons of confidentiality, we could not know who the siblings on the Register were and so, after a complex process of gaining permissions and setting up the necessary technology, it was arranged that respondents would make a free telephone call to the researcher, without divulging their own name or whereabouts, and that the call would be tape-recorded for transcription. There were far too many siblings potentially willing to be involved for an interview-based study to cope with, so a sample was constructed that would encompass the range of ages noted above, the proportion of brothers and sisters (roughly twice as many women, as is also found by post-adoption services), and the range of types of sibling relationships. Twenty-four interviews were completed and analysed thematically.

Selecting from the richness of material that resulted, this paper will report on the broad patterns of loss spoken about by birth siblings, illustrated by some of their individual experiences. This is perhaps the most important issue for current practitioners and policy makers to think about when faced with hard placement choices. The personal accounts in this study demonstrate clearly that severance is a two-way process; it is not only the child placed for adoption who undergoes a loss, but also the family left behind (or born later). Within this can be recognised in birth siblings some of the same needs and issues that have long been understood in relation to birth mothers and adopted people, together with some additional ones that are peculiar to their own circumstances. The length of the (lost) sibling relationship – throughout a lifetime – is one of these special aspects, as is the meaning of being a sibling as opposed to some other degree of relative.

In particular, this summary will focus on:

- the broad context in which loss of a sibling (or siblings) occurs;

- the meanings of "siblingness" and of adoption as perceived by birth siblings;

- the meanings of loss in relation to this;

- the impact of agency responses on loss.

The context of loss and the range of sibling relationships

Respondents had experienced a range of care models that reflected a diversity of family forms, as well as engagement with the public care system. Furthermore, because these arrangements had often been put into place in the context of family upheaval or trauma, they did not necessarily remain fixed throughout childhood which created yet further layers of complexity.

These shifting family patterns, in turn, gave rise to a multiplicity of sibling relationships. These ranged in status from "full" to what we decided to call "maternal" or "paternal" siblings (rather than "half-sibling", which sounds like an incomplete person), and to adoptive and step-siblings – as well as non-siblings who were nevertheless referred to as siblings. Beyond this, there was a further possible categorisation from enduring to non-existent or lost relationships, and some participants experienced separation from more than one sibling, through adoption and other avenues, simultaneously or over time.

The rather long account of one participant reflects particularly well this complex context of loss:

> Well, my mum died when I was 9 – I had a brother of 3 and a sister of 8 months old at the time – my brother and I were fostered for 3 years and then my father remarried and my brother and I went to stay with him and my step-mother but, unfortunately, after about 6 weeks it was

obvious, you know, that she didn't want children and we were put into a children's home where we stayed for several months, and then my real mother's brother found out we were in this home and made arrangements to visit us and a few months later we went to live with them – but, in the meantime, my sister (who was a baby when my mother died) stayed with the uncle I now refer to as my parent – my father gave permission for them to adopt her but then, out of the blue, he just refused to sign anything and she was sent off to someone else for adoption – we never saw her again. Then my father took my brother back and he and I lost contact for 21 years. I told him I was looking for our sister and he had no knowledge of her at all. I regard my cousins as my sisters – although they are full cousins, I just automatically think of them as sisters.

By a wonderful coincidence, this woman, aged in her 30s, had traced her full sister on the very day she was interviewed for the research.

Those on the Register were no more or less keen to effect a reunion according to their degree of relatedness. Reference to "half" siblings seemed more significant to agencies than to individuals; participants explained that they often had to define or clarify a relationship to the authorities in the context of searching, but that it did not matter to them personally. To the majority of participants, loss was more significant than status – the majority saw the adopted person simply as a sibling who was lost. Thus, considering oneself as a sibling not only survived separation, it could also take on a special significance in that context. For "full" siblings, it was as if their status afforded "added value" rather than altering these fundamentals. It was something considered worthy of mention by those participants who possessed this status who, in interview, described their adopted sibling and themselves as "true", "proper" or "real" siblings and not just "bits or halves". Again, it could also be relevant in relation to outside agencies. These particular respondents sometimes used "full sibling" status as a lever with which to assert their "rights" to searching and, they felt, to contact.

"Siblingness" and loss

Other than awarding siblings a definitional place in families, we know very little about – or are unable to articulate – what "siblingness" means in terms of roles and relationships. As researchers, we have invented this rather ungainly word, "siblingness", to refer to the perceived meaning(s) of being a sibling as opposed to the externally perceived biological and social aspects of sibling relationships. But, although we explored this concept in some depth with participants in our study, we are unable to offer a single definition. There was too much contained within the concept.

In the narrowest sense, siblings were described in terms of a blood-tie – and the significance of this should not be underestimated. Most commonly, however, siblingness was described as a shared history and, certainly, if we measure significance in terms of longevity, sibling relationships are the most significant in our lives:

It's a very deep and meaningful relationship ... one, you know, is the longest you will ever have in your life with anybody – and one of the most changing relationships as well – the rivalry tends to go and something deeper comes in.

Furthermore, the concept of siblingness has to be gendered if we want to embrace all the meanings of sibling relationships:

I always did, when I was younger, want an older sister. I have a friend I've known since I was five and she's got two sisters and, you know, there's such a strong theme – I mean, I've got these three friends and I would say they are what I regard as sisters – I've told them absolutely every last secret I ever had. I think, with a sister, they have known you from when you were small so they know everything. I could confide in my brother but I always get the male perspective back – sort of a more practical view – but, there you go, I got a brother and that's that.

Whilst siblings lost to adoption may not seem to fit readily into these definitions of siblingness as rooted in shared history and shared relationships, the loss itself can become a shared history in that birth siblings recognise it as a two-way process. Many in the study referred to the loss to the adopted person of the birth family they did not know, as well as to themselves. For themselves as birth siblings, the loss of the sibling relationship was expressed and experienced in a range of ways. Feelings of grief, anger, resentment and even betrayal were associated with participants' discovery, memory of, or parting from the person who had gone to be adopted:

I can remember the day she was actually born – she was born at home and we were all in the house. I have memories of pushing her in the pram – going in before I went to school to look at her in the carry-cot – she was at the stage where, soon as she saw me, she knew who I was; there was recognition there, even though she was only a small baby.

The childhood memories often stayed with people so that, rather like birth mothers (see, for example, Winkler and van Keppel, 1984; Ward, 1991; Howe *et al*, 1992; Wells, 1993), siblings were left with a sense of unresolved grief.

Years went by and then I said to my own daughter – 'I've often wondered what happened to her'. I mean, this is the thing, I keep seeing this baby in a basket.

Other participants had no memory of their adopted sibling and, of these, some had discovered their existence in the context of a personal trauma such as a bereavement. Others gave accounts of finding out as a result of "chance conversations", "rumour" or through agency "indiscretions". Other participants, who were adopted themselves, discovered siblings lost to separate adoptions in the process of their own attempts to trace their birth families. Birth siblings' accounts went as deep as those of adopted people in other studies (Triseliotis, 1973; Haimes and Timms, 1985), with participants describing a sense of devastation or disbelief at the discovery of a sibling, as well as a sense of relief at the confirmation of a vague sense of knowing there was "something" that had not felt quite right or had been hinted at in family conversations or silences.

But loss that had been rooted in the "immediate" became multi-dimensional with the passing of time. Lost siblings became lost aunts and uncles to the next generation; their children became lost cousins to respondents' children. In this way, the shared history that was described as representing siblingness became not only a lost past and a lost sense of the self as a sibling in the present, but also a lost future. This multi-layered loss was expressed as something that was not easily resolved, even with reunion:

> *People should think more about the ongoing effects – on the rest of the family or the family they have in the future.*

> *I don't think the kids could actually understand why one minute they didn't have this Aunty and the next they did.*

Parental qualities of loss

Because loss of a sibling becomes transgenerational in this way, connections with parenthood often feed into motivations to search. As with many adopted women, for female participants in our study, becoming a mother themselves had often forged both a commonality with their own mother and an associated awareness of her grief at relinquishing a baby.

Again, the parental theme is multi-layered. Certainly, some respondents were encouraged to search by their birth mothers and others, though acting independently, felt they were doing so on behalf of their mothers. But other participants who conducted searches for their siblings were motivated by the parental-like aspects of the sibling relationship itself (whether these were real or ideal). One man described how:

> *I used to look after him – feed him, change his nappies, things like that. I was about 12, I think, and I came home from school one day and he had gone. That's all I can remember.*

And a woman who had had no contact with her lost sibling expressed her anxieties in words that echo many accounts in the literature from relinquishing mothers (including in Mullender and Kearn, 1997):

> *If he knows he's been adopted he may wonder why he was given away. I would like to try and explain to him that he wasn't just abandoned – that he was wanted.*

The meaning of adoption

The sense of stigma associated with adoption as a social phenomenon was absorbed through a range of experiences.

I remember when I was a kid at school there were a couple of children who were, you know, like that [i.e. adopted] and they used to get teased about it. You know, kids are cruel aren't they: 'You're adopted – you haven't got a real Mum and Dad'. Never knowing the circumstances [of having an adoption in own family].

Some participants, of course, could draw on their own experiences as adopted people. Others contrasted adoption with their own disjointed family life.

As far back as I can remember, no matter where I was living or who I was living with [among extended family], I never felt part of a family. I remember [some carers she was placed with outside the family] having an argument in my presence because he wanted to formally adopt me and she didn't. So this word "adoption" sort of suddenly reared its ugly head, and then I realised that people who were adopted were taken by people who wanted them. I felt reassured when I learned that my brother and sister had been adopted, but it raised a question mark about me.

Because it was in their history, and had often involved a woman unable to keep a baby by reason of poverty or stigma, almost all saw adoption as outdated. The significance of adoption as a form of loss is enmeshed in the legal and social network that surrounds it, and, in this context, the negative response of agencies to the desire for reunion often accentuated the sense of loss, isolation and stigma that birth siblings experienced.

The experience of searching

The shared history of loss of each other is often not recognised by practitioners (and certainly not by the legal system) unless both siblings have been adopted separately or, at least, neither has been raised by birth parents. Some participants found that these circumstances-in-common (as opposed to shared circumstances and history) evoked a positive response from agencies when they embarked on their search.

They said that the fact I also hadn't been brought up by my parents was helpful. I wasn't adopted but we were in the same boat.

There were two examples in the study where a practitioner appears to have breached policy in favour of a recognition of siblings' moral rights to contact.

One bit of paper that a social worker sent me had my sister's adopted name on it. The social worker who was working with me said she'd never known that mistake before but she said 'Jolly good luck to you'.

My daughter's mother-in-law works for the council and had many contacts. I'd already written to the welfare in the area [where] my sister was adopted, with not much response. But my daughter's mother-in-law did a bit of asking for me and this kindly lady gave me the information on my sister she had. She gave me her adopted name. She said it couldn't hurt anybody because it was thirty-odd years ago.

But these were the exceptions. Most participants, even those who were adopted themselves, met only with negative responses.

Overall

The significance of the loss of a sibling is as broad, deep and complex as sibling relationships themselves. In social work there is a tendency to associate these relationships with childhood, but the experiences of the participants in the study reported above indicate that separation from siblings needs to be understood as it relates to the whole life-cycle.

> We've grown up apart and we shouldn't have done. We shouldn't have been parted. We could have been friends and we've missed out on all that.

Clearly, then, from looking at these experiences of the past, we can see the significance of decision-making about families and about placements for children in the present.

Looking wider: common themes from a range of work

There is a tension between the significance we know the loss of a sibling can hold and the complexities of family decision-making. Children may have a whole range of sibling and sibling-like relationships as their families change and fragment; they also continue to build new relationships when they go into extended family, adoptive, foster or institutional care. These include attachments to adoptive parents' birth children and other adopted children in the same family (Selman and Mason, 1999, forthcoming; Wilkings, 1999, forthcoming – all references in this section are to chapters due to appear in Mullender, 1999, forthcoming), and to other children in residential settings who may become a kind of "serial step-family" (Horrocks and Milner, 1999, forthcoming). For black children, there are wider resonances still in addressing others as brothers and sisters, for example, in Asian families and in the African Caribbean community (Prevatt Goldstein, 1999, forthcoming).

Despite moves away from closed adoption, separation from siblings and from other children who have been experienced as significant is not a thing of the past, as work by Marjut Kosonen, Beth Neil (both 1999, forthcoming) and others clearly shows, even to the point where, according to Kosonen, neither the child nor his or her social worker may know all the other members of the family, let alone where they all are. How is the practitioner to find a way through all this?

Fortunately, amongst the confusion, there are some useful pointers. First, a truly child-centred approach is to start from children's own understandings of who their siblings are and of which children (siblings and peers) are significant in their lives, ensuring that these are recorded on file. They also need regular updating. Even poor sibling relationships may improve when each child's needs are being fully met in placement, and they can also be worked on with help from the social worker and/or carers. Second, children can be kept in touch with news of all their relations. Third, placement decisions and contact arrangements can be made with reference to child–child as well as adult–child relationships. We know from Kosonen that children do value being placed with their siblings; they also worry about separation. Even if there are particular siblings with whom they do not want to be placed, they want to be nearby, and they think about sharing activities with their brothers and sisters right through into adulthood.

Yet Kosonen found that children's wishes are often not reflected in their current placement circumstances. Worryingly, too, Selwyn (1999, forthcoming) tells us that children are still not being properly enabled to express their views. Many simply do not appear to have been asked directly what they want to have happen. There is a tendency, too, to treat a sibling group as a unit, melding together what each child may have said into one combined comment, and blurring it still further with what adults think and with what has been happening in the children's lives.

Not everything children say they want will be possible. There remains a shortage of placements for sibling groups and of policies emphasising their importance (Beckett, 1999, forthcoming), though participants in the 1998 Symposium were able to report some successes in placing groups of as many as five children together and this was excellent news. There may also be many other ideas that could be tried. Siblings might go into the same placement but sequentially (e.g. Elgar and Head, 1999, forthcoming), thus reducing the strain on each other and on the rest of the family. Or siblings could be placed individually with single adopters who have the networking skills to maintain close links between them whilst sustaining a single-minded focus on each child's needs (Owen, 1999, forthcoming). Or there might be ways of offering additional support to the sibling who is going to find it most difficult to trust and to settle, often the oldest one (c.f. Wilkings).

Of course there are particular issues involved in placing children who have exhibited inappropriate or abusive sexual behaviour towards their siblings or other children (Elgar and Head, Farmer, 1999, forthcoming). Here, safety needs must predominate. But, with caregivers sometimes not even being told that abuse has taken place (Farmer), we cannot currently claim to be meeting the needs either of the young perpetrators or of those they may abuse in the future. If caregivers were adequately informed of the circumstances and supported in providing close supervision, this might mean that contact between siblings could become perfectly possible for many children.

Conclusion

The one simple message from all of the above is that all placement and contact decisions need to take the impact on sibling relationships over a lifetime into account, and to involve children as partners and as experts in their own lives. There are also some more detailed lessons, as outlined below.

Summary of common themes

Sibling separation:

- risks deeply felt and long-term loss

- is still very common

- may happen by default (e.g. through lack of a policy or of suitable placements)

Complexities:

- are present in complicated family structures

- make it hard to say what exactly is a sibling

- mean we must look hard at who are children's significant other children, including peers and not just siblings

Obstacles and challenges reside in:

- a lack of clearly delineated policies

- well meaning but sometimes confused practice

- the need to disseminate new research findings quickly

- the need to channel resources into finding sibling group placements and into maintaining complicated contact arrangements

Good practice with children:

- gives children a voice (who is in their family; who is significant to them)

- values child–child relationships (siblings and peers)

- records family changes

- records children's perceptions and wishes

- is aware of the individual needs and wishes of each child (including safety)

- never closes the door on contact (including in later years)

- is not satisfied with a "snapshot" assessment since feelings and relationships can change over time

- does not mistake sibling rivalry or conflict for not caring (now and later)

- works on problems in sibling relationships/does not write them off

- helps peers ("quasi-siblings") keep in touch after care

Good placement practice:

- recruits more families for sibling groups

- innovates (e.g. making sequential placements; rethinking the approved number; trying cluster arrangements across families, including with single carers; single carers taking sibling groups; calling on the extended family)

- gives full information about children's experiences, needs and wishes to carers

- ensures that carers also value child–child relationships, both existing and created

- supports contact arrangements (including with cash where possible)

References

Beckett, S. (1999, forthcoming) 'Local authority planning and decision-making for children', in Mullender A. *op. cit.*

Elgar, M. and Head, A. (1999, forthcoming) 'The placement of sexually abused and abusing siblings', in Mullender A. *op. cit.*

Farmer, E. (1999, forthcoming) 'Sexually abused and abusing children: their impact on "foster siblings" and other looked after children', in Mullender A. *op. cit.*

Haimes, E .and Timms, N. (1985) *Adoption, Identity and Social Policy*, Aldershot: Gower.

Horrocks, C. and Milner, J. (1999, forthcoming) 'The residential home as a serial step-family: acknowledging quasi-sibling relationships in local authority residential care', in Mullender A. *op. cit.*

Howe, D., Sawbridge, P. and Hinings, D. (1992) *Half a Million Women: Mothers who lose their children by adoption*, London: Penguin.

Jones, A. (1999, forthcoming) 'The achievement and sustainability of sibling contact: why the reality falls short of the ideal', in Mullender A. *op. cit.*

Kosonen, M. (1999, forthcoming) ' "Core" and "kin" siblings: foster children's changing families', in Mullender, A. *op. cit.*

Mullender, A. (ed) (1999, forthcoming) *We are Family: Sibling relationships in placement and beyond*, London: BAAF.

Mullender, A. and Kearn, S. (1997) *"I'm Here Waiting": Birth Relatives' Views on Part II of the Adoption Contact Register for England and Wales*, London: BAAF.

Neil, E. (1999, forthcoming) 'The sibling relationships of adopted children and patterns of contact after adoption', in Mullender A. *op. cit.*

Owen, M. (1999, forthcoming) 'Single adopters and sibling groups', in Mullender A. *op. cit.*

Prevatt Goldstein, B. (1999, forthcoming) 'Black siblings: a relationship for life', in Mullender A. *op. cit.*

Selman, P. and Mason, K. (1999, forthcoming) 'Sibling relationships in families adopting a child with Down's syndrome' in Mullender A. *op. cit.*

Selwyn, J. (1999, forthcoming) 'A "forever and ever family": siblings' views as represented in reports for adoption hearings', in Mullender A. *op. cit.*

Triseliotis, J. (1973) *In Search of Origins: The experience of adopted people*, London: Routledge and Kegan Paul.

Ward, D. (1991) 'Closed adoption – a lifetime loss', in Mullender A. (ed) *Open Adoption: The philosophy and the practice*, London: BAAF.

Wells, S. (1993) 'Post-traumatic stress disorder in birthmothers', in *Adoption & Fostering*, 17 : 2, pp.30-32.

Wilkings, J. (1999, forthcoming) 'Adopting siblings: my experience', in Mullender A. *op. cit.*

Winkler, R. C. and Van Keppel M. (1984) *Relinquishing Mothers in Adoption: Their long-term adjustment*, Institute of Family Studies Monograph No.3, Melbourne.

Experiences of transracial adoption

DEREK KIRTON
University of Kent
DAVID WOODGER
Association of
Transracially Adopted
People (ATRAP)

The research reported here stems from a pilot project undertaken with a view to more extensive research for which we are currently pursuing funding. As such, the report is essentially one upon work in progress, highlighting issues and lines of enquiry rather than offering "findings" *per se*. Although what we have to say is therefore necessarily tentative, we would still hope to make a contribution to ongoing debate in this contentious area. The research team comprises two representatives (David Woodger and Sue Jardine) from the Association of Transracially Adopted People (ATRAP) and two University-based researchers (Derek Kirton and Joan Fletcher, University of East London) and we would wish to acknowledge both the contribution of our two colleagues and the various supports offered by the Post-Adoption Centre to the work presented here.

Background

The driving force for this project has been our shared view of the limitations of existing research into transracial adoption (TRA) or the adoption of black and racial minority children into white families. These limitations relate particularly to the prevalence of "surface level" investigation, deriving from a combination of the sensitivities of the topic (with its emotionally charged cocktail of "race", family and adoption) and issues of methodology. As is probably well-known by those in the field, the broad message emerging from research into TRA has been of its general "success" along with a tendency towards "white" orientations on the part of many, probably a majority of adoptees (Feigelman and Silverman, 1983; Gill and Jackson, 1983; Bagley, 1993; Simon *et al*, 1994). While most studies have acknowledged that parental practice in relation to issues of racial identity, heritage and dealing with racism has often been less than ideal, the resulting deficiencies have rarely been portrayed as significant for adoptees. This picture was sufficiently at odds with our experiences drawn from various sources to act as a spur to conduct our own research. Our "scepticism" was also fuelled by evidence, from those rare studies which have probed a little more deeply, of the greater pressures and difficulties associated with transracial adoption (McRoy and Zurcher, 1983; Howe and Hinings, 1987).

The prevalence of relatively superficial analyses of TRA reflects two major factors. The first is that most studies have focused their efforts on gauging "success", employing what appear to be the most objective measures, such as psychological tests, self-esteem inventories and the like. It is our view that these devices are not well-placed to pick up the highly nuanced experiences of transracial adoptees. While qualitative interviews offer more potential for exploration of the issues, most research to date has involved one-off interviews of children/young people by strangers. This context is unlikely to be conducive to open discussion of what are both extremely sensitive trand personalised issues. The net effect of such problems is likely to be one of under-estimation of the additional challenges involved in TRA around issues of "race" and racism. Beyond methodological limitations, it is also important to remember that research into the experiences of transracial adoptees in the UK remains very limited in scale, and particularly so in relation to adults. Publication of the Department of Health-sponsored study (Thoburn *et al*, forthcoming) will offer the first qualitative research into such experiences but also serve to highlight the need for further research.

Aims of the research

In broad terms, the project aims to address the problems outlined above, namely the lack of research into (adult) experiences of transracial adoption in the UK, and the methodological limitations of research into TRA more generally. Our particular focus is on exploring questions of racial identity, cultural heritage and racism in the lives of black and racial minority adoptees in white families. More detail on research methods is given below, but particular features are those of linking the process of sampling to systems of existing contact and support and attempting to maximise the involvement of participants in the shaping of the research. It is hoped that this will result in the research being both supportive and providing a greater voice for transracially adopted people in relation to research and ultimately, policy and practice in this area. In sum, the aims would be i) to significantly extend research into the experiences of transracially adopted adults and ii) of transracial adoption in the United Kingdom, iii) to offer a more detailed examination of the issues of racial identity, cultural heritage and dealing with racism, iv) to provide a more supportive environment for such exploration and its follow-up, and v) to promote good practice in the placement of black and racial minority children.

Research methods and sampling

The major research methods are those of individual interviews and follow-up group discussion, although only the former have taken place within the pilot project. Interviews have been carried out in pairs, with a gender balance and at least one ATRAP member. A semi-structured schedule has been used with the aim of combining and balancing the concern for clear focus with that of facilitating exploration of the key issues identified above. The schedule is divided into four main sections, dealing with biographical data (including details of birth and adoptive families, circumstances of adoption, life events, etc.); racial/ethnic identity; culture and heritage; experiences of racism. To conclude, interviewees are invited to comment more directly on transracial adoption, both from their own point of view and more generally.

Within the main sections, the emphasis is on mapping the nature and salience of identity, culture, and racism in the lives of adoptees. The questions are designed to draw out patterns of continuity and change over time, the complexities and ambivalences surrounding "race" and adoption (but often suppressed in research and debate), the significance of particular racial or ethnic boundary markers, and the contexts for experience, whether more localised and immediate (e.g. family, close friends, school, neighbourhood) or broader (social changes, politics of "race"). The follow-up group discussions will have a dual purpose. This is first to allow reflection(s) upon the individual interview process itself and second to discuss further some of the issues and themes emerging from those interviews. This includes debate on transracial adoption itself and should provide an important channel through which adoptees could express their views in a more "collective" environment. It is envisaged that the discussions will involve roughly 5–6 people in each group. Throughout the project, there will be an emphasis on feedback to, and dialogue with, participants in the research, some of whom will also act as "readers" of draft reports.

In terms of sampling, the longer term aim is to carry out at least 40 interviews and for most of those interviewed to participate in the group discussions (though this is not a requirement). The sample will be drawn primarily from within ATRAP's membership, but will include some participants known or contacted via other organisations e.g. Post-Adoption Centre, The Children's Society, and Independent Adoption Service. The nature of this sampling clearly means that those interviewed cannot necessarily be taken as "representative" of a wider population of transracially adopted people i.e. they have approached particular organisations for one or more services such as information, support, mediation or counselling. However, for several reasons, we believe it would be quite wrong simply to dismiss the experiences narrated as "unrepresentative". For instance, most of those interviewed to date (and those to be so in the future) would probably fit the "success" criteria widely used in adoption studies – holding good jobs, presenting well, etc. They are also known to hold diverse views on transracial adoption and could in no way be characterised as "embittered". In the case of ATRAP, while some members join as a result of difficult or even damaging experiences, others do so for reasons of social contact with others from similar backgrounds and may be equally involved in giving as in receiving support. It is also important to recognise that there is no neat boundary to be drawn between those who approach organisations and those who do not. This may depend on contingencies such as information about, and perceptions of, the organisation and the individual adoptee's own strategies, coping mechanisms and so forth. There may also be psychological and social barriers to making approaches. One of our interviewees spoke of feeling "disloyal" to her parents, while another's partner had said of his membership of ATRAP, 'I don't know why you want to be part of that, you haven't got a problem'. Whatever the arguments over representativeness, we believe that any potential disadvantages are more than offset by relationships and familiarity which create the context within which people can be more open about their experiences.

Preliminary findings and emerging themes

The findings reported here come from ten interviews and as such must be treated with great caution. However, despite the small number and the question of representativeness referred to above, the accounts given in these interviews do not suggest that experiences were highly atypical. Most adoptive family circumstances fitted the pattern of TRA, of upbringing by "liberal, middle class" families, usually with other children (birth and sometimes adopted) in the family, and living in predominantly white areas. It is also important to emphasise that most of those interviewed paint a picture of loving, well-intentioned parents and childhoods which were happy in many, if by no means all, respects. Thus, while personalities and dynamics in families obviously have a significant impact on experiences, the difficulties described by adoptees cannot be explained in terms of family "pathology".

Before concentrating on those aspects of transracial adoption which proved particularly difficult for adoptees, it is important to note some of the positive aspects. Most acknowledged the value of stability and family support, not least in areas such as education. More directly connected with issues of "race" and ethnicity, some also felt that their highly unusual "vantage point" had provided elements of diversity, special insights and certain "freedoms" associated with their particular upbringing and environment. However, such positives were also recognised in part as coming to terms with the difficulties of belonging to "white" society or to their own "communities of origin". To highlight these issues is not to promote an image of inevitable "marginality" for transracial adoptees, but to give expression to feelings which can easily remain hidden. Adoptees also spoke, explicitly and implicitly, about their resilience in meeting complex and often painful challenges, whilst expressing a wish that this had not been necessary.

Virtually without exception, interviewees expressed the view that they had been brought up "white" i.e. with little recognition of their racial or ethnic identity, or deviation from white British mono-culture. Equally, almost all felt themselves, to varying degrees, uneasy in their relationship with "whiteness", an unease which most could recall wanting at some points during childhood or adolescence to resolve by becoming white. The sources of discomfort included those which have figured in most studies of TRA – the visibility of adoption, looking different, constant questions and the need for explanations, being the only black child in a school class, or the position of being an "honorary white" yet being on the receiving end of racial abuse, albeit often in the guise of "banter". Subsequently, with the development of racial and ethnic identity and increasing understanding of racism, these factors tended to crystallise into a clearer sense of not being white, but in turn raised issues of relationship both to "whiteness" and to alternative reference points.

Not surprisingly, the major reference point was that of the racial or ethnic identity of birth parents. In this, albeit tiny sample, black or racial minority identities tended to prevail over white identities for children of mixed parentage, perhaps reflecting on the one hand, the former's social significance and pejorative uses and on the other, its potential value as an identity source. Relationships with adoptees' own "communities of origin" tended to be highly complex and to give rise to ambivalent feelings, on the one hand exerting a powerful draw yet on the other representing uncertainty, and sometimes even threat. The ambivalence was detectable in accounts of childhood encounters (usually fairly isolated) with those from ostensibly similar ethnic backgrounds. Almost invariably, the latter took on a special significance, but this was sharply polarised, sometimes a force for attraction, but more often one for avoidance or rejection. The challenges surrounding relationships with "communities of origin" appeared to reflect various factors. These included awareness of negative stereotypes, which could stimulate avoidance either directly or indirectly through fear of association. More powerful influences came from feelings around "authenticity" and fear of rejection.

Notions of "authenticity" in relation to identity and culture have become distinctly unfashionable, viewed as oppressive manifestations of "political correctness" in a globalised world where identities have become highly fluid and increasingly "chosen". While there are elements of truth in this depiction, it is easy to forget that expectations of what it means to be "Indian", "Chinese" and so on remain powerful. The challenge facing transracial adoptees is one of being identified (and probably self-identifying) with a particular ethnic background, yet in many respects neither feeling nor acting in line with that identification. A recurring theme for interviewees was that encounters with members of their own communities evoked simultaneous and often profound feelings of being both "like" and "unlike" them. 'I'm black British, but I'm not black British'. The prospect and sometimes the reality of being rejected as "too white" was particularly hard to bear first, because (re-)connection with the community was often of particular importance to those who had been adopted away from it and second, because acting in ways which were simply the "natural" product of socialisation in a white family/community might be cast as conscious distancing from or even "betrayal" of ethnic identity. Such barriers are not insurmountable but from the evidence of our pilot research seem to demand "hard work" (often meaning a sustained period of "immersion") while yielding mixed results, some adoptees feeling they had established a satisfactory relationship with their "community of origin", others less so.

Attempts at engagement on the level of "culture" produced similarly mixed results, sometimes rewarding, sometimes painful. On the positive side, it could bring entry into a very different world yet one with which adoptees tended to feel a powerful connection. 'To identify a link beyond my actual years of life, the sense that there is a tremendous rich culture in which I have a part'. Yet "culture" in its various forms could also present barriers, perhaps from an inability to speak an "expected" language or attending "cultural" events, classes etc. as someone new to the particular cultural form in question, or simply a sense of viewing the world in very different ways. Though now in a different context, such factors could again lead to feelings of being exposed and dilemmas over disclosure. None of those interviewed felt they had been given any significant "cultural input" by their families. Where efforts had been made, they appeared limited, and were consequently often experienced as counter-productive. 'There didn't seem to be any meaning behind it'. Our research to date also tends to suggest that it is "lived" rather than "museum" culture which is sought by adoptees. Although this might have an historical dimension to it, it is the sense of connection with contemporary communities which seems to matter. This is important to set against critics of same race policies who often claim they are backward-looking, searching for some "primordial" view of ethnic identity.

Given the difficulties experienced in relation to racial and cultural identities, it is not surprising to find that adoptees had felt largely unsupported in the face of racism. Most described quite extensive experiences of racial abuse as children giving way to more institutional racism in adult life. Several had had experience of racism in the extended family and some regarded their adoptive parents as racist, albeit rarely in very overt ways. The pervasive colour blindness in most adoptive families seemed to have had the effect of closing communication channels. Sometimes this was the result of parental responses to reported incidents, but often arose from a perception that they 'wouldn't understand'. Interviewees also spoke of having 'protected' their parents from the racism they experienced, and sometimes of internalising it. The factors influencing communication, or lack of it, cannot of course, be explained simply in terms of "race" but it was also clear from adoptees' testimony that the absence of a shared experience of racism was a significant obstacle. Interestingly, virtually none of those interviewed regarded their parents as unaware of racism. Rather, it was that for the most part, they did not appear to connect this with their children's experiences, or were unable to communicate an understanding. Although aware that such issues are always potentially difficult to discuss, most adoptees felt this would have been much easier in a family of similar racial or ethnic background. This was supported by their experiences with friends, for while most had some white friends with whom they could discuss racism, this was generally easier with those who were felt to have similar experiences and understandings.

Implications for assessment, preparation and support

Drawing implications from our research presents certain dilemmas in relation to the themes of this symposium. Having looked at experiences of transracial adoption, it might seem logical to consider how preparation and support for it can be improved. We will offer comments below on this (particularly in respect of existing placements) but must preface this with our major observation, namely, that the difficulties highlighted in our research underline the need for vigorous pursuit of placements which are matched in terms of "race" and ethnicity. This applies both to domestic adoption and to inter-country adoption, which, if it is to be supported as a matter of public policy rather than viewed simply as a private activity, requires attempts to engage with communities based in the UK e.g. the Chinese community for children being adopted from China or Hong Kong, etc.

The picture which is suggested by our research is one where there are deep-seated difficulties for white families in meeting the needs of black and racial minority children in relation to issues of identity, culture and racism. While good preparation and support to existing (or future) placements is clearly important, their potential to compensate for other shortfalls must not be over-estimated. It is our view that those white families which might successfully meet children's needs in these areas are very rare and likely to have highly unusual experiences and skills. In particular, it is important that they have engaged in some depth – involving close interpersonal relationships in a multiracial context – and have gained a confidence in dealing with these issues which is also rooted in a deep appreciation of their significance. Crucially, this must entail reflection on "whiteness" and its central importance within the adoptive situation. Both awareness and the ability to communicate (in its broadest sense) that awareness are vital. The ability to steer a course between "avoidance" and "over-zealousness" demands a particular kind of openness, but this should not be confused with the kind of liberal "open-mindedness" which can easily co-exist with relative ignorance of the significance of "race" and racism. Most commentators now recognise the importance of families living in multiracial areas where the children will have a wider range of experiences and potential supports to draw upon. However, living in close proximity is not sufficient, and it would be necessary to gauge the nature of the family's particular network, whether of extended family or close friends. Clearly, these are matters for assessment, but in the context of the enormous challenges involved, we would emphasise the importance of any adopters having a "track record", rather than simply a "potential", in dealing with the issues.

For the reasons stated above, we would not suggest linking these issues to preparation – any conceivable "preparation" offered by an adoption agency would only serve, albeit indirectly, to give the impression of their relative superficiality. We would see preparation more in terms of helping applicants apply their existing understandings to the particular situation of adoption. This would need to be done both generally and specifically in relation to any child with her/his own unique life history. Given the many complexities of adoption, questions related to "race" and ethnicity must be carefully interwoven into any preparation, which, in turn, underlines the need for strong baseline understandings. Our view of support follows a similar rationale. Once again, the nature of adoption, irrespective of any racialised or ethnic differences, requires strong support services – whether practical or financial, the availability of advice, counselling and so forth. However, as with preparation, no supports, existing or foreseeable, can make good deficiencies which are rooted in the experiences of adoptive parents. It is also important that the requisite assessments, preparation and support are undertaken by those, from whatever ethnic background, who are equally experienced and skilled in dealing with issues of "race" and ethnicity and able to relate them effectively to the context of adoption. Finally, within the agency and its culture, there must be a demonstrable, incorporated understanding of the issues and ongoing commitment to providing the necessary supports. Again, it is important to reiterate the point that this constellation of factors is extremely rare in contemporary Britain and its child care services, and thus to underscore the continuing need for "matched" placements. Paradoxically, those agencies which best fit these criteria may also be those which are most effective at recruiting black families and hence make little or no use of transracial adoption.

There are, of course, many existing transracial placements where these stringent criteria have not been met and it would be naive to imagine that none will be made in future. We would hope our research can contribute to an understanding of the likely areas of difficulty in relation to issues of "race" and ethnicity. The need for strong post-adoption support is, of course, widely recognised, but we would see the area of transracial placement as one where this is particularly so. Where "race" is the focus of work, it will inevitably be challenging and it is important that agencies are as proactive as possible in offering support. As our research has shown, assuming "no news is good news" can be dangerously misleading. While individualised forms of support may often be appropriate, the potential for the shared experiences of groups should not be overlooked. Albeit by the nature of our sampling, we were talking to adoptees who had found the mutual support of ATRAP particularly valuable. What seemed most important was the sense of having extremely unusual circumstances and hence of finding people with whom many elements of them could be shared.

Meeting other people within the group I'm constantly being amazed by the similarity of experience.

I think it has been very good for me to explore it with someone who has been there and therefore understands exactly what I am on about, with so much not needing to be explained just comprehended straight off ... that has been absolutely invaluable and I treasure it.

Some had also found groups and individual counselling offered by organisations such as the Post-Adoption Centre very supportive.

Finally, although our research does not deal with "same race" adoption, the findings highlight the challenges inherent in adoption, and serve to warn against any view that matching provides a panacea. Issues of racial identity, culture and racism are highly complex and challenging to all parents and children. Although it is likely that black parents will be better equipped to meet children's needs in these areas, this must be carefully assessed, and backed up by appropriate preparation and supports. Thus, the comments made overleaf in relation to professionals and agencies are equally applicable.

References

Bagley, C. (1993) *International and Transracial Adoptions: A mental health perspective*, Aldershot: Avebury.

Feigelman, W. and Silverman, A. (1983) *Chosen Children: New patterns of adoptive relationships*, New York: Praeger.

Gill, O. and Jackson, B. (1983) *Adoption and Race: Black, Asian and mixed children in white families*, London: Batsford.

Howe, D. and Hinings, D. (1987) 'Adopted children referred to a child and family centre', in *Adoption & Fostering* 11 : 3.

McRoy, R. and Zurcher, L. (1983) *Transracial and Inracial Adoptees: The adolescent years*, Springfield: Charles C Thomas.

Simon, R., Altstein, H. and Melli, M. (1994) *The Case for Transracial Adoption*, Washington D.C.: American University Press.

Thoburn, J. *et al* (forthcoming) *Permanent Family Placement for Children of Minority Ethnic Origin*

Kinship care: Enabling and supporting child placements with relatives and friends

BOB BROAD
Senior Research Fellow
Department of Social
and Community Studies
De Montfort University
Leicester

Introduction

Against a background, at a national level, of concerns about the quality of care of children living away from home (see, for example, Berridge, 1997; Berridge and Brodie, 1998), especially those leaving care (Biehal *et al*, 1995; Broad, 1998) and locally, the search for more responsive and effective child care strategies to complement hard pressed foster care services (especially a shortage of foster placements for 14–16 year olds), child placements with relatives and friends, appears another, and potentially more positive, alternative for children living away from the parental home.* Also at the local level, and for the research project, the London Borough of Wandsworth had a range of important concerns about the nature and extent of this work, including the costs and benefits involved, how placement decisions were made (and on what basis), what local authority support is made available to relatives and friends, practitioners' views, and, not least of all, how the local authority's policies and practice match up. In terms of the legislation there is also statutory encouragement for placements with relatives in that the Children Act 1989 states that unless it 'would not be reasonably practicable or consistent with his welfare', it encourages placement of that child with a person connected with that child: a family member or relative, or 'other suitable person' (Children Act 1989,Section 23[6]).

Research aims and methodology

The initial aims of the research were to identify the number and type of child placements with relatives and friends in the London Borough of Wandsworth for a specified period, January 1992 – December 1996 (in the absence of a comprehensive information system having the capacity to provide this information). More specific aims focused on practice and management issues including: reporting on the costs involved in this work, exploring professional decision making and the way the local authority's policy was working, and identifying agency concerns about placement and assessment practice. The research then set out to meet these aims and begin to answer these questions through pro formas as well as a structured questionnaire sent to social workers and team managers. An advisory group was set up to manage the research. There are three phases to the research:

- Phase 1 – this phase recorded the situation regarding the number and type of temporary and permanent family placements of all cases for a four year period from January 1992 to December 1996. This "audit" phase of the research was undertaken in 1997 by means of a pro forma sent out to all social workers and managers identified as being involved

---

* In this paper the working definition used for the term 'child placements with relatives or friends' is 'of a child living away from the parental home and coming to the attention of the local authority to be placed either on a temporary or more permanent basis'. These placements usually involve a relative or friend of the child(ren) asking the local authority for some sort of assistance or arrangement, including, possibly, making decisions about legal orders, financial, and social work support.

in this work. The identification of workers involved in this work proved very time consuming.

- Phase 2 – This more complex phase explored professional practice and policy issues by sending a questionnaire to each of the social workers involved for each of the 116 children identified in Phase 1. Undertaken in 1997/98, this phase produced a response rate of 62 per cent with 70 completed questionnaires returned. SPSS for Windows software was used for data analysis.

- Phase 3 – Undertaking interviews with a sample of relatives, friends, and children is at the planning stage.

The local authority policy framework

Underpinning and guiding social work practice and its management in Wandsworth are the local authority's policy and procedures. In its *Children and Families Manual* there is a specific item entitled "Accommodation and placement with relatives and friends" concerning policy, selecting legal options, and financial authorisation and procedures (London Borough of Wandsworth, 1996). The section titled "Selecting the legal option" includes the key points that:

- The department must be satisfied that the proposed arrangement is in the child's best interests, including the child's racial, cultural, religious and linguistic needs.

- Responsibility for selecting the legal option belongs to the parents and prospective carers, but is shared with the department when the child is on a Care Order.

- The aim of selecting the legal option should be to empower the prospective carers and to minimise the department's role in caring for the child . . . consistent with the first point above.

- Residence Orders will generally be the preferred option for placement with relatives and fostering should only be considered when the . . . Residence Order has been ruled out.

In the section on assessment there is a strong emphasis on restating the council's preferred option of Residence Orders for placements with relatives, and finally, and at some length, the policy document states the position regarding the procedures for authorisation, payments and checks. It is the stated policy of the London Borough of Wandsworth's social services department to target resources at those most in need. Its policy is to try to keep children with their own family or existing social network, where this is consistent with its duty to ensure children do not suffer significant harm and that the child's welfare is not seriously prejudiced. Budgets are limited and it is acknowledged that difficult decisions often need to be taken between competing needs. The scope of the policy about financial support for friends and relatives is described as follows:

All families have crises where there is a problem about short-term care of their children. Many families sort out such situations without reference to the social services department. It is not possible to provide financial support for all families who experience crises in the short or long-term care of children, and the policy is to target resources on those families where support is necessary, and as an alternative to accommodating the child. It is not the department's policy to automatically offer financial support to assist relatives and friends to look after another person's children, and we should avoid the Department being perceived in this way.
(London Borough of Wandsworth, Social Services Department, 1998)

In the London Borough of Wandsworth the Section 17 budget is available to fund child placements with relatives and friends. It is stated that financial support provided is based on Income Support levels and the policy states that payments will usually be at 1.5 times the level of Income Support and may, in exceptional circumstances, be up to three times the level (London Borough of Wandsworth, 1996). Here, therefore, the organisation of the local authority's financial policy supports, to a point, the funding of child placements with relatives.

Summary of research findings

In terms of the age of the children recorded at the time of placement (n=60), 22 or 37 per cent were between 0–5 years of age, 16 or 27 per cent were between 6–10 years old, and 22 or 37 per cent were aged between 11 and 16. There were no children described as being over 16 years of age and overall there were the same number of girls and boys in the sample. In making comparisons with age groups from two other "populations", namely, all children in the Borough, and children looked after by the Borough, it was found that the age distribution of children placed with relatives and friends was very similar, in percentage terms, to both these two populations, at least for two of the three age groups. The exception was in the 0–10 year old age group which accounted for 57 per cent of all children placed with relatives compared with just 36 per cent of 0–10 year olds looked after by the local authority (London Borough of Wandsworth, 1997). This difference can be explained by local authorities not choosing institutional care as their first choice for younger children, and of course the development of placements with relatives and friends.

In terms of the ethnic origin of the children in the study, the two most common ethnic groupings, taken from the completed local authority's race monitoring forms, were "Caribbean or Guyanese", accounting for 31 per cent of all responses and "more than one ethnic group" [Non-European] and "other", also accounting for 31 per cent of children. Children of 'English, Welsh or Scots' ethnic origin accounted for 27 per cent of children.

There is then a much higher percentage of black children than white children being placed with extended family members although until the research is complete the reasons for this will not be known. By examining local looked after children data (London Borough of Wandsworth, 1997), it could be seen that there was a much higher proportion of black children

(33 per cent) placed with extended families, than black children being looked after by the local authority (24 per cent).

Further research would uncover other information and relay experiences. For example, in the first instance, comparisons with the London Borough of Wandsworth population as a whole would be helpful in establishing the facts about the different ethnic groups in the borough. It is also possible that this higher proportion of black children being placed with relatives could be a "good thing", a "bad thing" or something of a "mixed blessing". What constitutes these positions depends on what they mean, who is articulating them and why. For example, theoretically, on the one hand, the higher proportion of black children placed with relatives may be a "good thing" in the sense of diverting and preventing even more black children entering the looked after system, with the accompanying unsatisfactory outcomes, as well as costs. On the other hand, the higher proportion could be a "bad thing" if black children and families are being inappropriately encouraged and channelled to take up a particular type of extended family placement, with or without supports, at the same time being denied other services. We would need to ask these families, through the further research planned, the reasons for their involvement with Wandsworth social services department and their experiences of the same. There could also be a "mixed picture" of experiences. The literature in the child care field already indicates an over-representation of black children in residential care in some local authorities (for example, Barn, 1990). Also, according to McFadden's account of kinship care studies in North America, relative placements, to use her phrase, for 'children of colour' are rising (McFadden, 1998). Thus the outstanding research questions to be addressed here, as well as broader policy questions, include those which, in Phase 3 of the research project, explore and record black children's and carers' experiences. This will complement the empirical data presented here, and make a vital contribution in its own right.

In terms of the ethnic origin of children and carers, and deriving from the child's immediate family, there was, somewhat obviously, a very high level of matching, in terms of the ethnic origin of both child and carer: 85 per cent of the children of Caribbean or Guyanese ethnic origin were placed with carers of Caribbean or Guyanese ethnic origin, with the remaining children being placed with carers identified as being from "more than one ethnic group" (non-European); 89 per cent of the children identified as "English, Welsh, Scottish" were placed with carers of the same ethnic origin.

The two most common previous placements for all the children placed with relatives, immediately prior to their current placement, were: "at parental home" – accounting for 41 per cent of the total, and "accommodated in foster care" – accounting for 24 per cent of the total. In answer to the question about the legal situation of the child prior to the current placement by far the most common was "none", i.e. no legal order – these answers accounting for 50 per cent of the total (n=62). The second and third most common prior legal situation was "Section 31 Care Order" and "Section 20 in need" accounting for 14 per cent and 13 per cent respectively. The remaining 12 per cent of cases were subject to Section 38 Interim Care and Supervision Orders.

In terms of identifying where children were currently placed "grandparents" accounted for 39 per cent of all cases, and was easily the most popular placement for these children placed with relatives and friends. This was followed by "aunts", accounting for 26 per cent, and "friends", accounting for 11 per cent of cases (n=70). There was no pattern identified either in terms of the age of the child, ethnic origin, and where placed. There were no significant statistical differences in terms of "ethnic origin" and "who placed with in current placement", with grandparents and aunts being equally popular across the two most frequently listed ethnic origin categories.

In the questionnaire, the six placement categories offered to respondents which "best describe the nature of the current placement" were: "temporary placement with friends or relatives – 'arranged' by the Department but no legal orders"; "permanent placement with friends or relatives – 'arranged' by the Department but no legal orders"; "Residence Order – made or planned"; "fostering placement – temporary or planned"; "adoption placement – orders made or planned"; and "Other (please specify)". In terms of recorded placement types (n=69) the main findings were that the "Residence Order" category was the most popular, accounting for 29 per cent of placements, followed by "a temporary placement", accounting for 27 per cent of placements, followed by "a permanent placement", accounting for 17 per cent of placements. In terms of placement and age groups, the most popular type of placement category for 0–5-year-olds was "Residence Orders", for 6–10-year-olds it was "Temporary Placement" and for 11–16-year-olds (where there was a smaller number of responses) it was both "Residence Orders" and "Temporary Placements".

Financial support was provided by the department for the first three months for carers in 60 (86 per cent) cases (n=70). Although, as one might expect, the amount varied, this was within a fairly limited and clearly defined range of payment levels, in most cases related to twice income support levels. In terms of ongoing financial support provided it was found that in 63 per cent of cases (n=70) ongoing financial support was provided by the Department. Surprisingly perhaps, where ongoing financial support was provided, it was found to be evenly spread across all six placement categories specified. There was no statistically significant association between the ethnic origin of the child and the existence or level of ongoing financial support. Because the cost of funding a placement with relatives is paid for from the same budget as a residential or foster care placement, when placements with relatives are used as an alternative they are a demonstrably less costly way of meeting a child or young person's needs.

The research also set out to discover what guided social workers' decisions about the type of placement in which they were involved. Respondents were given a choice of nine categories (of consideration) and asked to rank them from 1 to 9 in terms of the first or "top" (i.e. overriding) consideration down to the "least important" consideration on the list. The nine categories were: "family choice", "costs", "best interests of child", "empower the family", "department procedures", "level of funding available", "all that was available", "what was most suitable", and "contact enabled with parent/other". Respondents were also invited to state if/when none of the categories was a consideration and asked to specify if an "other' category applied. As one might expect, the "best interest of child" category was easily the most popular and cited of all first ranked considerations, and listed by 79 per cent of respondents. The second and third most cited first ranked considerations, but receiving much less support were "Family choice", listed by 11 per cent of respondents, followed by "what was most suitable" category given in a mere nine per cent of all first ranked considerations.

Allocations, authorisations and checks on carers

The overwhelming majority, 72 per cent, of cases were currently allocated by the Department (n=69) and the child placements had been authorised, normally at a more senior level than team manager, by a social work manager, although others were made at team manager and adoption and fostering panel levels. The latter had given the majority of their authorisations for Residence Orders. In answer to the question 'What checks (e.g. police/medical/local authority reference/personal references) if any were made about the relative or friend or carer with whom the child was placed?' it was found that there were a number of checks made on carers in 68 per cent of cases. There were at least three types of checks (including police, medical and local authority checks) carried out on all ten children whose legal situation in the immediate previous placement was a Section 31 Care Order, and where the Care Order still seemed to be in force. In 20 (34 per cent) cases there had been no checks carried out on carers and the vast majority of these children were in the "temporary placement with friends or relatives – arranged by the department but no legal order" category, with the immediate previous placement being at the parental home.

Implications for policy and practice

These issues derive from the responses to an open-ended question about identifying practice and management issues, and are summarised, highlighted and grouped together here under headings about the role of social services, training, work with black families, and implications for policies.

The role of social services

- In direct work there can often be what was described by one respondent as an "unspoken view" of the social services department that when a family is arguing for more financial assistance the family is labelled as only being "after money" and their commitment to the child is also questioned. This can put the social worker in a difficult position when the family seeks an advocate and the department insists its policy is followed. In one case, that of a child aged 15 in the category of "a permanent placement with relatives or friends – arranged by the department but no legal orders," a fundamental issue, one at the core of this work, emerged. In this particular case, and according to the social worker involved, there was always a different view of the placement between the social services department and the carers. The social services department's view was that the placement was an alternative to care and that it was supporting the family's responsibility whereas the carers' view was that the child was seen as the legal responsibility of the department on whose behalf they were caring for him. To the carers, there was always a sense that the department was "cheating" them by not allowing them to have the same financial support as the allowance payable, in their words to 'proper foster carers'.

- There was concern expressed by a number of practitioners and managers that the local authority policy was restrictive in terms of levels of financial support available and specified entitlements, and that there was an irony when grandparents would not come forward because of lack of financial support and the children were subsequently placed in care, at considerably greater expense to the local authority. It is not known how often this scenario did occur or whether this revealed a deeper frustration about policy restrictions on flexible and professional discretionary decision making. In turn this reflects what might be called "value dilemmas" about, on the one hand, social work practice and, on the other, social work management. So, for example, several practitioners voiced a view that an acceptance that families try to do their best for children and that policies should reflect the local authority's commitment to empowering families and believing 'what they believe to be best for their children,' does not necessarily square with the agency's wider child protection responsibilities. Experienced practitioners and managers also saw how the professional relationship could clarify roles and responsibilities, as one worker expressed it about one case, through 'an honest open relationship with the family. Persistently engaging them in the options available to the local authority were helpful with the family in understanding what could happen if the parents could not care for the child.'

Training issues

- Clearer financial guidelines that can be shared with carers are required.

- Where a local authority social services department has an independent provider of residential care, there needs to be more consistent decision making whereby family members are involved in discussions and considerations.

- Skills in holding reviews of a family placement may need developing as well as appropriate recording, assessment and monitoring forms.

- When grandparents are involved, "therapeutic input" may be needed for them to help understand and break generational aspects

- Systemic family work, attachment theory, family review work, child protection, permanency planning, family therapy work, and counselling were all areas often listed by practitioners wanting to develop their knowledge base.

Extended family placements and black families

The following four quotations taken from four cases illustrate different professional aspects of working with black families, and point to the benefits of having a more positive, sensitive and informed attitude towards the potential contribution of black families in this work.

- 'It is possible that a black social worker may have been more able to engage the family as the network was predominantly white. Grandmother had feelings of being alienated. Paternal family felt the "white" social services department was discriminating.'

- 'A shared cultural background helped an open and honest discussion about the child's parents' inability to parent.'

- 'There was self-esteem and a better sense of identity to be cared for by their grandmother rather than in foster care or in a children's home (black/St Lucian ethnic origin) and there were few if any resources for five children – they have been cared for together – this was very positive.'

- 'It was very positive working with a black family, by making the most of the family's strengths – rather than seeing them as the "problem".'

Implications for local authorities' policies

- There can be a real tension between the social worker, their local authority, the carer, and the child about the nature of the relationship between the state (here the local authority of course) and the individual and the family where there is a child placed with a relative or friend. At times, and as this research has revealed, this tension manifested itself in disagreements about financial entitlements and levels of financial support. Local authorities will likely be pressurised to produce clearer financial guidelines to be shared with carers, but may argue that these placements do not warrant financial entitlements on a par with foster care allowances because they are fundamentally different. This then begs the question: To what extent can/should a Residence Order placement receive the same level of support and checks as a formal foster placement?

- In this emerging child care area, within a reputable local authority which has had a comprehensive policy in place for several years now, it could be argued that more consistency in decision making about these types of placements is needed in the future as and when this work expands and that more positive encouragement to use and support placements with friends and extended family is required.

- Local authority departments which do not make available their Section 17, or similar, budgets for relative placements may well experience difficulties in making such placements, thus reducing their child care options.

- The London Borough of Wandsworth, and indeed other local authorities, may wish to re-emphasise the contribution of family group conferences or family group meetings (as they are known in Wandsworth) given their role and the positive, though limited, use made of them in this work.

- Even in those cases where the local authority has helped to make some temporary arrangement between a child and a carer, and has no legal responsibility, and because a number of these placements had not been fully checked, as was shown earlier, it would seem prudent that these, as well as carers with children on Residence Orders, and others, have proper checks conducted on them.

Concluding comments

There are many important planning, policy and practice issues about child placements with relatives and friends which this research has identified and begun to address. The financial and associated welfare issues about the role of the state and local authorities are especially critical issues, but should not dominate the discussion. So, whilst policies and practices are being developed, what should not get lost along the way, are the principal ideas underpinning these placements with relatives. These are for a child or children for whom living with the birth parent(s) is no longer a possibility, for local authorities and families to fully and openly explore together, subject to proper checks and considerations, the possibilities for placing that vulnerable child or children within their extended family (and possibly, but likely to be less often, with friends), in order to maintain continuity of care, relationships, family responsibility and support, and sustain ethnic and cultural identities. Child placements with relatives and extended families offer a continuity of, and coherence in, relationships and identity often so cruelly severed through other options. Nationally this approach to child placements needs further work and sharing of policy and practice developments, funded research and evaluation, and dissemination and training, if it is to make the fullest positive impact on vulnerable children and families.

References

Aldgate, J. (1991) 'Partnership with Parents – fantasy or reality', in *Adoption & Fostering*, 15 : 2.

Barn, R. (1990) *Black Children in the Public Care System*, London: Batsford.

Berridge, D. (1997) *Foster Care: A research review*, London: The Stationery Office.

Berridge, D. and Brodie, I. (1997) *Children's Homes Revisited*, London: Jessica Kingsley.

Biehal, N., Clayden, J., Stein, M. and Wade, J. (1995) *Moving On*, London: HMSO.

Broad, B. (1998) *Young People Leaving Care: Life after the Children Act 1989*, London: Jessica Kingsley.

London Borough of Wandsworth (1996) *Children and Families Manual*.

London Borough of Wandsworth (1997) *Children Looked After*.

London Borough of Wandsworth (1998) *Financial Issues – child placements with relatives and friends*, mimeo.

McFaddon, E. J. (1998) 'Kinship care in the USA', in *Adoption & Fostering*, 22 : 3, pp 7-15.

Expert assessments in court proceedings and the implications for support services in planning for permanency for children

JULIA BROPHY

This session focused on a summary of findings from new research on the use of experts in care proceedings (Brophy, with Bates *et al*, in press). The aims were first, to address "received wisdom" in this field comparing common views with research findings. Second, to explore some issues surrounding social work practices where cases are referred to experts, in particular, looking at the use of comprehensive social work assessments prior to referral to experts, and third, to focus on a number of findings about the use of child and family mental health experts. With regard to this latter issue the session raised a number of issues for the role of child psychiatrists in an overall exercise of preparing and supporting children during moves towards permanent family placements.

The project from which findings were drawn included four studies (Brophy, Wale and Bates, 1999; Bates and Brophy, 1996; Brophy and Bates, 1999; Brophy *et al*, 1998) which examined a number of practices and procedures where experts are instructed. The studies identified that contrary to much received wisdom in this field not all expert evidence is complex and the majority of cases do not contain competing evidence filed by all three parties in proceedings. Only 18% of cases in a national survey contained expert evidence filed from all three major parties (ie: the local authority, the guardian *ad litem* and the parents). Moreover, in the survey most cases which contained expert evidence did not proceed beyond a care centre. Relatively few were transferred to the High Court (11%) and a substantial number (35%) remained in the family proceedings courts despite the existence of expert evidence (Table 4.3 in Brophy, Wale and Bates, 1999). However, changes to law and to practices and procedures have increased the need for certain types of clinical evidence. Thus, "medical" evidence (i.e.: reports from paediatricians, radiologists, neurologists, etc.) was unlikely to be the only expert evidence filed in cases. It was usually followed by mental health evidence and child psychiatrists were the major providers of expert evidence. In a national survey of some 557 cases (concerning just under one thousand children), reports from child psychiatrists appeared in 41% of all cases (Table 4.9 in Brophy, Wale and Bates, 1999). Moreover, indications are that where conflicts did arise between experts, these were most likely to arise between mental health experts (eg: between child psychiatrists and between child and adult psychiatrists) and much of the conflict focused on the most appropriate care plan in cases and not, for example, about whether or not a case met the threshold criteria for a care order (Bates and Brophy, 1996).

Although conflicts between experts arose in a relatively small number of cases, such cases do raise very difficult questions both for professionals and for courts. However, contrary to received wisdom the research identified that conflicts do not simply arise between the experts instructed by local authorities and those instructed by parents. A comparison of reports filed in the most complex cases in the survey (Figure 1 in Brophy, Wale and Bates, 1999) indicated that differences of opinion also arose between experts instructed by each of the professional parties (i.e.: the guardian and the local authority). In other words, experts instructed by parents cannot be simply dismissed as "hired guns", experts instructed by the guardian may also disagree with assessments/opinions of an expert instructed by a local authority. In complex cases a second opinion can be important and conflicts of view are not necessarily a "bad" thing (Tables 4.19 and 4.22 in Brophy, Wale and Bates, 1999). Both guardians and child psychiatrists saw opportunities for obtaining a second opinion through peer review as a very necessary part of proceedings; they are part of the process of "trying to get it right for a child" in part, by ensuring that the least detrimental alternative is identified.

Findings from three studies in the project identified that child psychiatrists are now expected to provide a "package" of information for the court. This information builds on social work information but it also provides a range of additional information which cannot be supplied by social workers. Psychiatrists saw their work as complimentary but also having an "added value" to that provided by social workers. Equally, child psychiatrists acknowledged that social workers provided a range of information which they could not (Brophy with Bates *et al*, forthcoming). However, indications are that some further thought needs to be given to the role, function and quality of comprehensive social work assessments (the "Orange Book" assessment) in the context of legal proceedings (Brophy with Bates *et al*, forthcoming). There were some criticisms of this work. For example, interviews with child psychiatrists revealed that in some proceedings these assessments had not been undertaken by local authorities prior to referral for a psychiatric family assessment. Where they had been undertaken there was considerable variation in their quality – some were described as excellent, others very poor. The range of information about a child and family could be incomplete and reports could lack information about what had been tried with a family prior to referral to an expert.

The research indicated that child psychiatrists are undertaking medico-legal work from a number of institutional bases with varying contractual obligations so far as work in the field of child litigation is concerned. Interviews with child and adolescent psychiatrists (Brophy with Bates *et al*, forthcoming) indicated that services are somewhat fragmented in this area with relatively few psychiatrists able to offer any ongoing treatment and support for children. Both local authorities and guardians sometimes instructed psychiatrists with a national reputation for work in child abuse/neglect. This practice, of using consultants who were not locally based (i.e.: not "local" to a family) and where local child and adolescent mental health services were limited, had clear benefits for the immediate case. However, as far as the development of a coherent, high quality, locally based child and adolescent mental health service (CAMHS) is concerned, it raises a number of problems.

First, when "national" figures are instructed few are likely to be able to offer any further treatment for children. Second, where further work with a child is recommended, local services may not have the resources/skills to undertake it. Indications are that in some cases there is also a dilution of recommendations in court reports because clinicians are trying to pitch their recommendations for treatment somewhere between what they consider to be clinical necessary for a child and what they know to be available in a local CAMHS. Third, this fragmentation of the current service raises important questions about clinical continuity for children who are subject to care orders and where the local authority plan is permanent removal from a birth parent or parents. Current practices indicate there is little room for continuity of clinical support for a child or for the adults and professionals looking towards permanency in future placement.

Discussion

A wide range of questions was raised in the following discussion and these included the following:

First, whether when instructing certain experts, local authorities considered the likelihood of (a) any need for therapeutic treatment for a child and (b) whether the person they were likely to instruct would be able to offer this treatment if necessary. Indications are that it was not necessarily a criterion at that point in a case, although local authorities are likely to be restricted by many of the factors which influence guardians in this area. For example, the research identifies that appointing someone who can offer some clinical continuity is a serious consideration for guardians, and they often wanted to instruct someone who could offer further treatment for a child if that was deemed necessary – 52% of guardians in the survey identified this issue as one of their criteria in appointing a child psychiatrist. However, practices indicated that this consideration often gives way to instructing someone who is experienced in litigation and particularly someone who will be "good in the witness box" and who is available at the time.

The research throws some light on the institutional/contractual obligations of child psychiatrists which currently preclude or severely limit a more coherent approach to clinical services in this area. Interviews with psychiatrists from a range of geographical/institutional locations did not locate services where a comprehensive package was being attempted, although certain individuals reported they tried hard to offer something and many said they would prefer to be able to offer further treatment as part of their service. The research makes a range of substantial recommendations for changes to policy and practice in this field (Brophy with Bates *et al*, forthcoming), and some further exploration work in this issue is also necessary. The introduction of the internal market in the NHS has not resulted in better services in this field for children, parents or professionals and although there are indications that the purchaser/provider split is to be abandoned, this move will not necessarily improve child and adolescent mental health services so far as child litigation is concerned. Questions about co-operation between authorities (social services and health) were raised but so far as s.27 of the Children Act 1989 is concerned, practitioners' views confirmed indications from the research. As one seminar participant commented: 'It's [s.27] regarded by social workers as a bit of a joke – it has no "teeth", there are no obligations, social services can ask but there are no skills or resources in many locally based clinics'.

A number of questions were also raised which broadly focused on whether experts really made a difference to cases and what light the research could throw on this debate. The research, particularly the studies which included interviews with guardians (Brophy and Bates, 1999) and with child psychiatrists (Brophy *et al*, 1998), was able to spell out what might be called "divisions of labour" in this area. Of particular importance here is first, the general package of information now expected of child psychiatrists (Brophy *et al*, 1998) and the timing of their instructions in cases (Brophy and Bates, 1998). Second, it is important to unpack the work of the guardian in complex cases and see how social work skills and expertise underscore his/her work at different stages of a case, for example, in deciding which experts are needed (in terms of both discipline and particular specialism), the content of letters of instructions (e.g.: what an expert can reasonably be asked to comment on) and importantly, how social work skills are then brought to bear in assessing the quality of any subsequent expert report. The studies were able to identify when and how different skills are engaged in the light of the new law (under s 31 (2) (a) (b) and (9) (b) of the Children Act 1989) and the need to look not only at current significant harm to children but also to examine the likelihood of future risk. In many cases when looking at the complexity of issues, the range of parental behaviours which give rise for concern and the need to judge a parent's willingness/ability/capacity for change, a clinical diagnosis and prognosis will be necessary.

Questions were also raised about the direct work with children undertaken by the guardian *ad litem*. Guardian participants in the seminar reported undertaking considerable work in this field. The research looked at this question in two ways: first, in the context of practices in case management as a measure against which to assess the work of others (Brophy & Bates, 1999). In complex cases indications are that the process of instructing experts gets underway fairly quickly in proceedings and leave (i.e.: court permission) for a child to be assessed by an expert is often granted at the first directions hearing. The guardian's own assessment of the child then becomes part of her tools for assessing the work of both social workers and other experts in child and family mental health but it is important to note that her own assessment of a child will not necessarily predate the first application for leave – indeed it is unlikely the guardian will have had time for much direct work with children prior to the first directions hearing. Second, the survey of training and support in the GALRO service indicated that communication skills for interviewing children and young people was an area where some guardians would welcome further training (Brophy, Wale and Bates, 1997).

The low use of joint instructions to experts in the survey sample was raised (Figure 1 in Brophy, Wale and Bates, 1999) and there was considerable discussion of the problems and benefits of jointly instructing an expert at different stages of a case. It was reported by one participant that in one area there had been a local practice direction to the effect that experts must be jointly instructed by all three parties in proceedings. Some concerns were expressed about this practice so far as the quality of evidence was concerned, the position of parents in cases, and the loss of the "critical factor" in proceedings. Earlier findings from the survey were again discussed with reference to the differences of view and opinion which can arise between experts and how useful that can be (Tables 4.19 and 4.22 in

Brophy, Wale and Bates, 1999). Questions were also raised about the needs and concerns which underscored this direction. In particular, it raises questions about the precise role and function of psychiatry in such cases.

References

Bates, P. and Brophy, J. (1996) *The Appliance of Science?: The use of experts in child care proceedings – a court-based study*, report prepared for the Department of Health, London.

Brophy, J. and Bates, P. (1998) 'The position of parents using experts in care proceedings – a failure of 'partnership'?, in *Journal of Social Welfare and Family Law*, 20 : 1, pp 21-48.

Brophy, J. and Bates, P. (1999) *The Guardian ad Litem, Complex Cases and the Use of Experts following the Children Act 1989*, London: The Lord Chancellor's Department.

Brophy, J. with Bates, P., Brown, L., Cohen, S., Radcliffe, P. and Wale, C. J. (forthcoming) *The Use of Experts in Child Protection Litigation: Where do we go from here*, London: The Stationery Office.

Brophy, J., Brown, L., Cohen, S. and Radcliffe, P. (1998) *Law and 'Medicine': Psychiatry at the Interface of Child Protection Litigation*, report prepared for the Department of Health (two articles are in preparation based on this study of the work of child psychiatrists).

Brophy, J., Wale, C. J. and Bates, P. (1997) *Training and Support in the Guardian ad Litem and Reporting Officer Services*, Department of Health/Welsh Office and the Thomas Coram Research Unit, Institute of Education, University of London.

Brophy, J., Wale, C. J. and Bates, P. (1999) *Myths and Practices: The use of experts in child care proceedings*, London: BAAF.

Where now for research on permanent family placement?

JUNE THOBURN
Dean of School of
Social Work
University of East Anglia

A comparatively large volume of research is about to be published or in the later stages of completion, some of it described in the papers presented in this volume. Before a new research programme is planned, these findings need to be absorbed. The over-view being prepared on behalf of the Department of Health by Professor Roy Parker is a welcome first step towards a more coherent research programme. It is likely to conclude that more is known about outcome than process, and that the opinions of adopters are more frequently reported than those of adoptees.

The study by Caroline Thomas and colleagues (1999, forthcoming) is an important addition to the literature on the opinions of young people, covering as it does the period up to and shortly after the making of an adoption order. The University of East Anglia study (1998) provides information on longer-term outcomes and opinions of young black people who were permanently fostered or adopted. However, even these small detailed accounts provide little information about social work **methods** and **practice** as opposed to process.

There is an urgent need for a longitudinal study involving large numbers (using both qualitative and quantitative methods) which follows a cohort of children joining permanent substitute families through into adulthood. An imperative for future outcome research is that cohorts should be large enough for different ages and circumstances of the children to be controlled for. Alternatively children should be "disaggregated", with small scale studies concentrating on children of a similar age with broadly similar characteristics. Several of the chapters in this volume describe such studies, most notably that of Alan Rushton which focuses on children placed in their middle years. In the meantime, it is important to ensure that those smaller-scale studies which have collected data on the children at the time of placement are "revisited" as the children grow up.

Since family contact after adoption involves a significant change in practice, studies of different sorts of family contact (between siblings, and between adoptees and their birth parents, other relatives and previous carers) are needed to match those taking place in the USA. Does direct contact become indirect over time and vice versa?

Beth Neil's (1999) longitudinal study of children placed under the age of three who have face-to-face contact with adult birth relatives could be complemented by studies of children who have indirect contact or none at all. Perhaps this cohort of early placed children could be combined with the cohort of British infant adoptees studied by the Institute of Psychiatry team as a comparison group for those placed from Romania (Rutter *et al*, 1998). It will be important to ensure that future longitudinal studies include detailed contemporaneous information on process and practice as well as on subjective experiences of growing up adopted and on outcomes.

Infant placements have long been neglected by British researchers and there is an urgent need for new work to report on longer term outcomes for the sorts of children now being placed. We need to know more about the impact on adoption work and adoptive parenting of "involuntary adoption". How, for example, do adopters tell their children that they were placed for adoption because their mother killed a brother before they were born? How has the important task of "telling" changed now that more children have some form of contact with birth relatives?

Turning to the substitute families, there is very little large scale outcome research on the characteristics which make some new parents more successful than others. There are suggestions from the qualitative studies that it is aspects of personality and relationships which make the difference between success and failure. These are particularly difficult to capture accurately in a survey which contains large enough numbers for statistical analysis. However, if longitudinal studies are to be undertaken, it is essential that researchers attempt to build into their studies descriptions of these less tangible parental attributes.

The satisfaction of adopters (and to a lesser extent foster parents) with the service provided is more frequently studied than is the satisfaction of the other members of the adoption triad. There is thus a risk that policy on process, practice and decision making will be based on the preferences of substitute parents rather than of the children or the birth parents.

A review of the research literature indicates that birth parents receive a generally poor service and that researchers have paid less attention to their opinions about the adequacy and appropriateness of the services provided. Some small scale studies and Social Services Inspectorate reports suggest a research agenda might focus on their response to services at the time that their children are placed (particularly when their consent is dispensed with); their reactions to direct and to indirect contact with their children after placement; and the long-term impact on them of having a child placed for adoption or permanent foster care. It appears, for example, that it is the birth parents who find least satisfaction in indirect contact arrangements, since they are the ones most likely to pull out of the commitment to maintain a long-term but indirect relationship. However, very little is known about the nature of practice which would make it more possible for them to continue to play a part in their children's lives, albeit from afar. Given the prevalence of indirect contact, such research is urgently needed.

As I have mentioned in the opening chapter, much more research is needed on long-term and permanent fostering, and also on "bridge" placements which will provide stability for as long as it takes to find the right substitute family. Those studies which suggest that foster families confirmed as "families for life" are more successful than placements with strangers should be followed up with studies specifically designed to provide further evidence on this important question.

Finally, and to bring us back to the recent Department of Health Guidance and the *Quality Protects* agenda, it is essential that new ways of working which are introduced with the aim of placing children more quickly (such as the "concurrent planning" experiment), are evaluated to check out that there are no unintended adverse consequences.

References

Neil, B. (1999) *Contact after Adoption* Newsletter 2, Norwich: UEA Centre for Research on the child and Family.

Rutter, M. and the English and Romanian Study Team (1998) 'Developmental catchup and deficit following adoption after severe global early privation', in *Journal of Child Psychology and Psychiatry*, 39 : 4, pp 465–476.

Thoburn, J. Norford, L. and Rashid, S. P. (1998) *Permanent Family Placement for Children of Minority Ethnic Origin*, Norwich: UEA Social Work Monograph.

Thomas, C. and Beckford, V. with Lowe, N and Murch M. (1999, forthcoming) *Adopted Children Speaking*, London: BAAF.